MW00912640

LEGENDS AND TEACHINGS OF

XEEL'S,
THE CREATOR

DR. ELLEN RICE WHITE – KWULASULWUT

WITH FOREWORD BY Dr. Jo-ann Archibald – Q'um Q'um Xiiem

ALSO BY DR. ELLEN RICE WHITE – KWULASULWUT

Kwulasulwut: Stories from the Coast Salish
Kwulasulwut II: More Stories from the Coast Salish

Legends and Teachings of Xeel's, the Creator

Dr. Ellen Rice White – Kwulasulwut

Foreword by
Dr. Jo-ann Archibald – Q'um Q'um Xiiem

Theytus Books
Penticton, BC, Canada

© 2018, 2006 Dr. Ellen Rice White – Kwulasulwut

First edition published in 2006 by Pacific Educational Press

All rights reserved. No part of this publication may be reproduced in any print or digital format without the prior permission of the publisher, or in the case of photocopying or other reprographic copying, a license from Access Copyright, the Canadian Copyright Licensing Agency.

THEYTUS BOOKS
www.theytus.com

Green Mountain Rd., Lot 45
RR#2, Site 50, Comp. 8
Penticton, BC V2A 6J7

The author would like to acknowledge the contribution made by the Canada Council of the Arts towards the preparation of this book.

Library and Archives Canada Cataloguing in Publication

White, Ellen, 1922-2018, author
    Legends and teachings of Xeel's, the Creator / Dr. Ellen Rice White, Kwulasulwut ; Rachel Taylor and Vicki White, editors

Previously published: Vancouver : Pacific Educational Press, 2006.
ISBN 978-1-926886-55-8 (softcover)

    1. Coast Salish Indians--Folklore. 2. Legends--British Columbia.
3. Coast Salish mythology--British Columbia. I. Taylor, Rachel, 1983-, editor II. White, Vicki (Vicki Eileen), editor III. Title.

E99.S21W493 2018   398.2089'9794   C2018-904838-7

COVER ILLUSTRATION: Daniel Elliott
COVER PHOTOGRAPH OF DR. ELLEN RICE WHITE: Martin Dee / UBC Telestudios
COVER AND INTERIOR DESIGN: Rachel Taylor

AUTHOR'S DEDICATION

My deepest love and gratitude to the ancestors for never forgetting the teachings of the Creator, and for the passing on of those teachings: my granny Mary Rice – Xalunamut, and her only brother Tommy Piell – Quyupulenuxw, my mom's mother Louisa Bob – Tsun'uylhaat, my mom Hilda Rice (née Wesley) – Qw'ustanulwut, and my dad Charles Rice – Kwulasultun. The ancestors called our Creator Xeel's. Xeel's made things new so he could help make life easier for the people and animals he called his children. Xi' means to appear suddenly before you. Xew's is to make things new. That is why they called him Xeel's.

Many thanks to Verna Kirkness, Jo-ann Archibald, Wilson Duff, George Clutesi, and Mungo Martin for their encouragement and support in the writing of this book, which has taken ten years from beginning to end. And to my daughter Victoria (Vicki) Eileen White – Qw'ustanulwut for finding the English words for me.

My undying love to T'iqwup, my late husband Doug White—who is still ordering me around from the other side.

Contents

THANK YOU SONG

Hay ch q̓a' Sie'miye?
Thank you honoured
One

Hay ch q̓a' Sie'miye?
Thank you honoured
One

O ho, ho-o uh ho, hey
The One Up High

O ho, ho-o uh ho, hey
The One Up High

THE ROAD OF LEARNING IS DARK AND NARROW

If you falter and you fall, you get embarrassed.
You jump up and look to see if anyone saw you,
you look around and you go.
What did you learn?
The only thing you learned is embarrassment.

When you want to learn,
when you fall,
even in darkness,
you feel it, taste it, smell it, thank it.
Then even in darkness,
you will see.

Grandpa Tommy

Foreword

Dr. Ellen Rice White – Kwulasulwut was born in 1922. She was from the Snuneymuxw First Nation, a Coast Salish People whose territory is located on the east side of Vancouver Island in British Columbia. Kwulasulwut means Many Stars. During her childhood, Ellen lived on a little island near Duncan, which is south of Nanaimo. Although its official name is Norway Island, everyone called it Rice Island after her father's family. Ellen's parents were Charles Rice and Hilda Rice (née Wesley), and her grandparents were George and Mary Rice. Ellen's Granny Rice and Ellen's grand-uncle, known as "Grandpa Tommy," taught her traditional teachings and many traditional stories.

In this book, Kwulasulwut tells four of those traditional stories handed down to her from her grandparents and their ancestors of the Coast Salish peoples of the west coast of British Columbia. She says, "I could never say these stories are mine or Granny's or Grandpa's. Everybody knows that long ago Xeel's, the Creator travelled from village to village. He would say, 'I am needed. I have to go.' These stories belonged to Xeel's and he told them to people during his travels. We have to remember that."

Indigenous people also travelled to different villages and shared stories during their visits. Over time, the stories may have changed a little in order to fit a particular context of storytelling. Nevertheless, the core of each story, along with its teachings and values, has stayed alive, waiting to be retold in new ways.

During her childhood and into adulthood, Ellen's family ensured that she thoroughly learned her ancestors' stories and cultural teachings. For this book, Ellen worked with her daughter, Vicki White, to document these four stories in written form to be accessible to many others. These stories are appropriate for youth and adults. The stories, and the teachings embedded in them, can help individuals address matters of the heart, mind, body, and spirit that arise at different stages of their lives.

In traditional storytelling settings, the storyteller and listeners shared cultural knowledge and ways of making meaning from stories. However, over the years, a disruption of this storied linkage occurred in formal schooling systems that did not value Indigenous knowledge and oral traditions. As a result, these stories and ways of knowing were excluded from the curriculum. Many teachers have not learned to use Indigenous stories in meaningful ways. Concerned that the readers of her book would not be able to appreciate and understand the stories without the cultural understandings associated with them, Ellen developed discussion sections for this book that follow each story. Cultural teachings and examples of understandings that Ellen attributes to the stories for present-day application are included in the discussion sections to give readers some ideas about making meaning from the stories. The discussion is in a narrative form, as if Ellen was speaking to the reader. Teachers will find the narrative discussion format very helpful for preparing them to develop their teaching strategies for the stories.

Whenever Ellen heard stories, she said that she had to "figure out what the story meant." In following the traditional manner of making story meanings to encourage students' thinking in today's classroom, she said, "I do not want students to be told what to write. They can figure it out for themselves." Her thoughts suggest that students could think about their behaviour in relation to the characters in the story—to learn from their mistakes and from their successes; to let their emotions be felt and to engage in problem-solving; and to let the stories heal their inner spirit.

Another concern that Ellen had was that readers would not understand the role of Xeel's. She said, "I tried not to think of the Bible for these stories." Even though Xeel's translates as "Creator" in the English language, it does not have the same meaning as "God" in the Bible. In Ellen's book, Xeel's means that new things came from existing things. Some form of energy created a new area or, in Ellen's words, "a brand new something happened" from an interaction with new energy. The stories in this book are examples of new things made from Xeel's energy. Another way to use new energy is to create individual and collective understandings or make meaning from the story. In the first edition of this book, Kwulasulwut encouraged each reader and story learner to use their energy through thinking, imagining, feeling, doing (writing, drama, art), dreaming, and talking to make new story meanings that were helpful and relevant to them.

Sadly, Ellen – Kwulasulwut passed away in August 2018, before this book was re-printed. However, her legacy is like her Indigenous name, Many Stars.

Throughout her lifetime, Kwulasulwut's teaching, mentorship, leadership, midwifery, and storytelling roles created sparkles of brightness and beauty, similar to the stars that one sees when looking at the night-time sky. Kwulasulwut was a dynamic community activist, dedicated Indigenous language linguist and revivalist, expert healer, and skilled educator; but above all else, she was a much beloved Elder, family, and community member. In her Elder years, Kwulasulwut continued to teach high school youth in university summer programs, and to mentor college and university students, staff, and faculty. Her numerous accolades and awards included: Nanaimo's Woman of the Year and Mother of the Year; BC Community Achievement Award; an honourary doctorate from Vancouver Island University; the Order of British Columbia; and the Order of Canada.

Enjoy and treasure the Indigenous stories in this book that Kwulasulwut has prepared so lovingly for you.

Jo-ann Archibald – Q'um Q'um Xiiem
Stó:lō and St'át'imc First Nations
Professor Emeritus, Faculty of Education
University of British Columbia

The Creator and the Flea Lady

EARLY IN THE morning before the sun came up, a woman was walking along the beach feeling very sad. She had a lot on her mind and tears were flowing down her face. When she cried, she felt very heavy. She was so little. She was the taʼtalhum lady—the flea lady.

She called out, "Please help me. You have spoken to me before. I know you are out there somewhere. You are in the water, in the air, in the sky, in the earth."

She was calling for Xeelʼs, the Creator. She was walking in and out of the qaʼ (water) talking to herself: "If only you were big enough… if only there was something I could do!" When the waves came in, they looked enormous to her because she was so small. The bubbles from the waves looked huge as they rolled onto the beach. She said to herself again, "If only you were big enough… if only I could help."

Then she heard a voice. "I am here, my daughter."

Before this she had not listened to Xeelʼs; she was not open to his teachings. But this time she listened. This time the desire to hear him was very strong. The voice said, "Listen to me."

She knew the voice and said, "Please help me, Father. If my baby does not get help, he will be gone by tonight. He is getting weaker all the time."

The voice said to her, "Keep on walking towards the bigger waves, my daughter."

She looked up and saw that there were bigger waves at the point. Every time the waves came, she could see the sand rolling up the beach, and the bubbles were getting bigger and bigger. She heard Xeel's say, "Look at them. See them." She looked and they were huge. She poked at one with her sharp fingers and it burst. She thought the breath it exhaled smelled very good. She remembered that smell; it was the same smell as when the healthy ones were born.

"Father, why am I smelling that familiar aroma?"

"Continue walking, my daughter, and you will see," he said.

By this time, she had stopped crying and thinking about how sad she was and how pitiful her little son was, lying there on a tiny leaf. His brothers were looking after him. They were sprinkling qa' on him so he wouldn't dry out. They called him the "unfinished one" because he was born early. You could see the ribs of the tiniest leaf right through him. Even when he was given a drop of water or milk, you could see it going all the way down into his little intestines. It was too awful; she didn't want to think about it.

"I am going to be strong because Xeel's, the Father, is here and I am not going to waste time feeling sorry for myself," she told herself. "Help me, Father, help me, please."

As she continued walking, she could see three bubbles rolling back and forth, seeming to change colour. Her thoughts were coming from deep inside her. "I am not going to worry. I am going to look at the bubbles. I am going to listen to Xeel's. Father, help me."

Now she could hear the bubbles moving back and forth, and it was as if the sand were talking to her. Her mind was communicating with the sand. All of a sudden, she felt happiness as she kicked the sand back and forth. She said to the sand, "I am very sorry. You were so happy. I didn't mean to disturb you." But she knew the sand was telling her it was all right. She was hopping now and it seemed like she wasn't in the water. Every time the water came she touched it. It didn't feel like water, it felt like skin.

She asked the water, "Are you all right? You feel different."

The water answered somewhere deep inside her. "We are here for you. We are happy for you."

When she heard that, she knew the sand was there to help her and her little transparent one. All of a sudden, everything became clear. She chose one big bubble which was almost over her head, and she danced around it. She touched the bubble to introduce her smell to it and it came towards her. She moved up to it and became braver, and when she poked at it, it didn't break. She carefully moved it out of the water. She said "hay ch q̓a', hay ch q̓a' (thank you, thank you)" many times. She made a little hole in the sand for the bubble and said to the sand, "Please look after it for me."

The sand was grunting and groaning as it moved around the bubble to hold it. She looked up and she could see that she wasn't far from home. She started hopping and it felt like she was floating, like she was flying. Her boys looked up and said to each other, "Mother is coming. She looks very happy." She kept waving at them but when she got closer, they said, "He's not breathing too well, Mother. We gave him more liquid but he isn't taking it."

She told them she had heard the voice and now she knew what to do. "I have found a bubble that we can put your little brother into and this will help him to live."

They became very excited. One of the boys said, "Mother, I feel something. I feel very happy."

She said, "I know, I feel happiness as well. You stay with your little brother and we will bring the bubble up here."

The boys began to run around excitedly. When they took the bubble, they remembered to thank the sand, and the sand said, "Remember, we can help you!"

The eldest boy said, "Mother, was it in my mind that I heard that? I heard, 'Remember, we can help you.'"

"I heard that also, my son. It was the same when the grains of sand helped me move the bubble out of the water. They helped me roll it right up to the shore and they were so careful when they moved the rocks out of the way."

The mother and son remembered to thank the rocks when they moved them, and the rocks became light as feathers. The young man kept saying "hay ch q̓a', hay ch q̓a'" and the rocks all kept helping.

"This will be the place. This place will protect us from the wind," Mother said. They made a hole in the sand and continued to talk to the sand; the sand grunted in reply. Mother was now very happy for her son. She kept saying, "Hay ch q̓a' for helping us." The grains of sand piled on top of one another, struggling to help. Finally, they got the bubble to where the little boy lay. Mother went to her unfinished one and said, "We have a home for you to be finished in." He blinked his little eyes and nodded to her. The other boys said, "He is smiling." They were all happy now.

There were relatives from far away who knew what was going on. They could feel that something important was happening. They started to arrive and you could see them hopping along, coming to be with the family. They stayed a distance away because they knew if they got too close they might spoil the communication, the connection, the magical powers, the spiritual powers surrounding the family. They said, "We will stay here and send our energy. We are thanking Xeel's, our Father, for you and your little one."

The mother looked at her eldest son, who was standing there waiting for direction from her, and she knew what he was thinking. It felt like everything was opening up and becoming clear.

"Mother, how are we going to get him in there?" he said.

She heard the voice in her mind say, "Remember the straw. Remember your own slime from your nostrils and your mouth."

She remembered a vision she had had a long time ago. In it, she had been crying, and her vision showed her stretching her baby in a straw. She had thought the vision meant that when he died she would put him in a straw and he would float away. But now she thought to herself, "This is what we are going to do to help him!"

She said to her sons, "You must go and look for a straw." One of the brothers found several straws and he brought them all in case one didn't work. She didn't question her son's thinking because they were thinking on the same level. It was as though they were in a fog, as though they were inside clouds, and they were all communicating together. Even the relatives outside the circle were in the same place. Some of the relatives had gone to sleep under logs and some had found food and were piling it up for when the work was done.

"Now we need tears," the flea mother said. She looked at her sons, who were already crying. The tears were rolling down their faces and then her own tears started to roll down her face. Because she loved her children so much, the juices from their noses came easily and mingled with the tears. They began to blow the warm fluid into the straw. They tried the smallest straw first and it didn't work, but the larger one did. The fluids started to flow right into the straw. She spoke to the bubble. "Accept this as food." The bubble was anxious to eat and let the straw in.

She looked at her unfinished one, rubbed her face, then rubbed his little body. The eldest son came and also rubbed his face and then rubbed his little brother's back. They rubbed and rubbed and it seemed as if he was starting to stretch. They spoke to the little one. Mother said, "Stretch your body, little one. Stretch your body. You must fit into the straw."

They had already blown some tears and the fluid from their mouths and nostrils into the bubble and they could see it dripping down the tube, making a bed for him in the bottom of the bubble. As she kept stretching him, his little face becoming longer and longer, she heard the voice say: "His face must be down. His face must be down, and his head goes in first." They turned him over and pushed him head first into the straw. The straw was creaking; it was comforting him and talking to him.

"Please help our little one," Mother said. "We love him so much and we need him." The straw got thicker and moister as they kept rubbing it with tears and saliva, and it expanded with the heat. They could almost feel themselves inside the straw—pushing. His little face went down into the tube and all of a sudden he floated inside. He lay on his side and turned onto his little back. It was as if he were lying on a feather bed but it was steamy and warm.

The family watched him inside and they were so happy. They said to the Creator, "What shall we do with the straw?"

"Leave it in and I will tell you when to take it out."

"Hay ch q̓a', hay ch q̓a'," they said to Xeel's, the Creator.

They watched for the longest time and the little boy's shape started to fill out, his little face getting fuller and his body starting to form. His body didn't look like a tiny piece of grass anymore. He was breathing so much better. He looked at them and smiled. He seemed to be floating.

The family hollered loudly, praying to Xeel's and thanking him. They sang the thank-you song and danced on the logs. When they got hungry, they ate from the food the relatives had prepared. The mother didn't want to leave her little one for too long, so she ate a bit and hurried back to him. When they could see the little one was getting dry and didn't have enough air, she remembered the words spoken by Xeel's: "You must blow air through the straw. Remember, he must also get to know someone else's breath." The mother told her eldest son to blow into the bubble. He thanked his mother for allowing him to do this and then he blew and blew. His little brother smiled and went back to sleep. They took turns blowing into the bubble that day, the next day, and the third day.

Xeel's, the Creator—the voice—was speaking to them. They called him "the voice" now because this was how he communicated with them. He said, "We must use others; there are others who can help."

There was a young woman who said, "I heard the voice." She asked if she could help and then she started to blow into the tube. After she got tired, someone else came to help.

The old people made a big circle and gave offerings. They brought food and laid it out. They said, "It is the smell of food Xeel's wants." They made a little fire and burned the small crabs and delicate ferns and flowers.

They didn't use the strong flowers but only the most delicate ones. The Creator thanked them for the smell of the food; he survived by the smell alone.

When Mother was alone with Xeel's, she whispered to him, "Can I help you?"

He said, "I only need very little liquid, very little aroma of the food. I don't take it away, I only use the aroma."

She said, "I am happy that you have what you need. I am going to partake of the food we have burned, but only after I know you have taken the aroma."

"Mmm, ahhh, hay ch q̓a'," Xeel's said.

On the fourth day the baby was rolling around inside the bubble playing. Xeel's said, "It is now time for him to come out of the bubble. You must soften the straw with fluids to prepare it for removal. You must also soften the bubble with fluids so it is easy to break."

The family listened to the instructions. They softened the straw and the bubble with more fluids, removed the straw, and then started to poke the bubble. All of a sudden the bubble burst and the baby tumbled out. The children quickly picked him up and they cried and laughed in happiness. Then the children gave him liquid by dipping their fingers in the juice from a clamshell. His mother rubbed his tiny body and fed him with ꞌeyꞌx̌alꞌlh, the tiniest little crabs. Those gathered could see that the little one was going to survive, and the old people said, "It is now time for us to leave. We are going to look for food. We must take the young ones with us as we need to look after them." There were many, many young ones.

Then the voice of Xeelʼs said from far away, "I am also leaving." The family cried, since they did not want him to leave. "If you cry for me, I will feel sorrow," he said. "If you don't cry, I will be happy when I leave." The flea mother and her children wanted to cry but instead they danced on the beach and ran in and out of the water. The little one also danced. They all looked up to the sky and held up their hands and said "hay ch q̓aꞌ, hay ch q̓aꞌ."

Speaking with Ellen about
"The Creator and the Flea Lady"

THIS LITTLE STORY is about life, death, and survival. It is the tale of the flea mother's journey from despair to success. She calls on Xeel's, the Creator in her time of need and learns how to use the energy of the universe found in the air, water, and earth. It is also a journey into the world of the newborn. Xeel's shows the flea mother how to put her premature baby in a bubble, an ingenious kind of incubator, to help it survive. Along with the flea lady, we learn that there is a time to seek the guidance of Xeel's, a time to listen to your inner self, and a time to be connected to your surroundings. There are many helpers in the universe if we acknowledge them and ask for their help.

The flea mother hadn't listened to Xeel's very well in the past because she was a very critical person— critical of him, and perhaps also of herself. She had not been open to his teachings. But now, walking along the beach and feeling small and helpless, she was able to remember something from the lessons of long ago: Xeel's would be there if she called him; she could go anywhere and he would hear her.

At last the flea lady called out to Xeel's, and he began to guide her. He directed her to listen and be aware and watchful—to think about the situation, to go inside herself and contemplate it. He told her to look at the bubbles in the surf. She broke one of them and smelled the smell that was released. The aroma brought back memories, a smell of long ago when she had her first-born. At that time, she had been directed to smell the baby, taste it, touch it, caress it so she would never forget. She had learned the lesson well.

The time she spent walking on the beach was very important because it led to her calling on Xeel's and to inner contemplation. At times in our lives it is important to be alone, to ask for help, and then to listen. As the flea lady made her connection to the spirit, she stopped crying. She stopped thinking about how sad she was and how pitiful her son was. She decided to be strong because Xeel's was with her and she was not going to waste time feeling sorry for herself. She moved from self-absorption and self-pity to thinking about a solution—from inaction to action.

She remembered to communicate with the sand, the water, and even the rocks. She asked for their help and thanked them for helping her. We might well ask, "How can they help if they are solid objects such as rock and sand?" Well, remember that rock and sand and water are ancient elements of the universe, created by Xeel's, the Creator of all things.

The universe is made of energy. All things, animate as well as inanimate, are imbued with it; and we are all connected by universal energy. Inanimate things such as rocks, snot, and saliva may have a different kind of energy, but it can be potent—if you believe. Our own energy works with the energy of things that we can touch, both solid and liquid. We can ask these substances to transmit their energy and direct it towards helping us.

The flea lady's relatives arrived to help. They knew that something was happening because they could *feel* it. They knew that it was important to go to the family so they could support it, but not to get too close. Long ago, people were more in tune with one another. They were knowledgeable about communication and energy because that teaching had always been passed on to the young, and the knowledge was not lost. In today's world, however, we still work with energy, though we may not be aware of it. We do this with our brain and with our very being. Sending energy to others is easy if you understand how. We may think that we don't know how to do this, but we do. Isn't prayer this way? Have you ever prayed for help because you wanted to help someone else?

When the flea mother was crying and feeling sorry for herself, she was closing her ability to receive energy from other sources. In her mind, her son was already dead. But when she asked Xeel's for help, she remembered a vision she'd had long ago, of stretching her baby in a straw. It was this vision that gave her the idea of what to do.

Before you make a decision to act, an original thought forms in your mind. This is the strongest thought because this is when you are first calling the energies to help you. The thought becomes a vision in your mind and then you can actually go ahead and act on it.

One way we can make use of the elements is to think about the setting, the surroundings, and which elements might be able to help. Take the birth of a baby. You do not want people running in and out of the room. You want to create a calm, welcoming atmosphere. It is important for the family to be in the same energy—like the flea lady's relatives who felt as though they were inside a fog, or perhaps a cloud, along with the baby and his family, all communicating together.

When we are present at the birth of a baby, it is as though we and the mother and baby are all inside a dome or a bighouse and we don't want to disrupt what's at the center. It is important for everyone to be in the same energy, the same mind, asking for the same thing, all in the natural flow. If it is a dry birth, perhaps we can think about fluids, such as wet snot and tears, to help bring forth liquid to the birth canal. We can bring these substances to mind and then transfer that thought to the body in need. We only need to ask for their help.

The baby flea was in the same dome with his family and relatives, asking for the same thing, all in the natural flow. Putting the little one through the straw wasn't easy, but they persisted, asking him to help them by stretching his body. They kept rubbing the straw with tears and saliva and the heat expanded it. They were helping him; they became one with him. It is the unity of thought that is important, the prayers, the sharing of the energy.

In the story, the family and relatives were all there helping and observing as the little boy's shape started to fill out. Babies are very delicate and dependent on the adults around them, so it is important for a family to watch closely. Is his face getting fuller? Is her body growing and forming properly? When the flea mother noticed that the little one was getting dry she immediately knew what to do. You, too, can ask yourself questions such as: "Is the baby receiving enough stimulation? Is the baby receiving enough food and liquid? Is the baby too hot? Is the baby too dry?"

For three days, they blew air and fluids into the bubble, then Xeel's said that they must find others who could help. This is the teaching: we should use others to help. There are times when we need to depend on others; for example, if we are alone with a new baby and don't know what to do. We watch the baby—the eyes, the tongue, the nose. If we haven't had a baby before, we might not know if its progress is normal. Does the urine smell right? Do the feces smell right? Does the baby have a healthy smell and look? At times, we just need to ask for help.

The old people wanted to make offerings of food to Xeel's, and they knew it was only the smell of the food that Xeel's wanted. The knowledgeable people said the aroma of food is powerful. A long time ago, you would never see a mother carrying a baby around food, especially strong-smelling foods. Xeel's says babies can smell and taste the differences in food even before they are born. The midwives taught new mothers that the unborn can smell, taste, hear, and feel. Pregnant women were taught what to eat and how to behave during pregnancy; for example, not to eat strong-smelling food, not to be around ugly things, and not to be around people fighting. The baby can feel all of this while it is in the womb, and it is already learning. We can endanger the future of the baby if we are not trained to abide by the rules.

Now that the baby was happy and healthy, it was time for the relatives and Xeel's to leave the family. Instead of crying because Xeel's was leaving, the family followed his suggestion and danced on the beach instead. In today's world, this teaching is still valid. If we cry for someone who is very ill and we are in sorrow, that person will feel there is no hope, as though they are already dead. If we cry for a sick baby, the baby feels it. The mother is supposed to be very happy as she builds the liquid inside herself to feed the baby. If the mother is unhappy all the time, the baby will also be unhappy. You should overcome your sorrow to help others. It teaches the young mother that care must be taken from the very first month, since the baby is already aware and learning.

This story offers many lessons about survival and how to ensure the success of your offspring's life, and the lives of generations to come. It teaches us that we must never stop asking questions; we must work at using the teachings for the betterment of our own future and that of future generations. Through the example of the flea lady, this story shows that we can ask for help, we can ask for a situation to change— but it takes work and perseverance.

The Boys Who Became a Killer Whale

A GROUP OF young people was gathered at a private meeting place far away from their village. It was a special place where they went when they had concerns they didn't want the Elders to hear. These young people, who had not quite reached the age of puberty, were upset that they were not included with their older brothers and sisters during the teaching time and felt they were missing out on the sacred teachings.

A boy named Shuyulh, which means "the older one," led the group. Shuyulh and his three younger brothers were always first to arrive at their special meeting place and they made a fire. No one spoke until they were all gathered. They knew how to conduct themselves as they sat around the fire. They waited until everyone arrived, and then the older one looked up and nodded to them.

The younger ones who did not know what they were meeting about thought, "This is very, very serious." As young as they were, they knew the difference between the time to talk and the time to be quiet. They all felt the heaviness and waited for direction.

Shuyulh looked at them and said, "We are all gathered here today because of the way we have been treated. We are not babies anymore. Our parents and the Elders ask us to get wood, look for pitch in the woods to start their fires, search for special types of wood for barbequing, gather special rocks for pit cooking, and do other things such as getting water or berry juice for the Elders. They do not have to tell us how to do these jobs because we already know how. They have taught us these things many times.

"But why is it when they address problems or teachings, we are sent away? When we are learning how to soften the inner cedar bark and we are doing it the right way we are included, but if we do anything wrong we are told to go away."

One of the young cousins spoke next, saying, "One time I cried for a long time after being yelled at and I fell asleep behind our bighouse. One of my older sisters found me and brought me inside and told everyone how she had found me.

"An Elder questioned me and I told him I was just tired and had fallen asleep. The Elder asked, 'Why are your eyes swollen? Why have you been crying?' I told him I had made a mistake and broken the inner cedar bark while I was preparing it for rope. I offered to do it again and make another one. I said I would keep it soaked so it would be pliable and not break, but my uncle took all the inner cedar bark away from me and said, 'Just go away. Stay away from here.'"

The young cousin continued. "Then we all heard a big voice from up in the sky say, 'Have you forgotten the teachings of the Father?' The Elders said this was the voice of the Creator. One of the Elders then told my uncle, 'You have to watch what the children are doing. You must teach them. They have to learn how to do it right.'

"But my uncle didn't offer to show me how to do it right. So I asked my grandmother and she said, 'You have to go and ask the adults. It is their job to teach you. I can't help you right now, but if the adults tell you to come to me, then I will help you.' The adults were working on the bighouse and I went to them even though I was afraid, but they told me to go away."

Another cousin agreed. "I couldn't swallow my food for two days when I thought about what happened to me. Why do we think about these things while we are eating? I can't swallow my food when I think about it.

"I was one of the people making rope. When we finished the rope, we tied the planks with it and hauled the planks up to the roof of the bighouse, but the rope snapped. The planks came tumbling down and we scrambled away. One of my cousins wasn't fast enough and a plank hit him. He was crying and I wanted to cry with him. One of my uncles said, 'You children go away from here. Don't offer to help anymore until you learn to do it properly.' We said, 'Tell us how to do it properly, then.' My uncle replied, 'You don't speak to the rope, you don't honour it. You do not respect it. You are just playing. That is why the rope got angry and broke.'"

Then a girl shared a similar experience. "While we were helping to make baskets one day, the adults told us to wash and separate the inner cedar bark and to make long strands from the roots of the stinging nettles. We didn't know we should make both long pieces and shorter pieces, so the longer and shorter pieces can be twisted together into one. The long pieces kept breaking and separating and we just let them break. When we gave our older cousins the rope to finish the basket, they said, 'This is too short. Why is it so short?' They didn't tell us how to make the long and the short strings so it would be strong.

When they used the basket to haul rocks up to the roof of the bighouse, the rocks came tumbling down on us because the fibres were weak.

"They blamed us and told us to go away. We came here that day and we dug up some roots, some fern roots, and that is all we ate all day. When we went home we could hear them teaching our older sisters and brothers. We crept closer and closer and when they saw us they told us to go to the far end of the bighouse. Then we couldn't hear what was said."

Shuyulh spoke next. "My three brothers and I were talking about this and I was selected to crawl under the steps of the le:lwusl (seating place). I was able to stay there for a long time listening. My older brother is only a year older than me but he was allowed to be there. My eyes became accustomed to the darkness and then I saw other eyes and recognized chuchíʔqun, mink. Mink just stared at me, but I was too busy listening to pay attention, until I realized mink was also listening. Was he curious or did he want to learn, like me?

"The Elders were talking about the importance of 'speaking' to the materials you are working with. It is important to talk to the trees when they are standing and to the bark when you are separating it from the tree. It is important to honour the tree and the bark.

"The Elders also talked about tumulh (red ochre), which they put on their faces when they dance. They talked about how they use qa' and about the different uses of fresh water and salt water. They discussed how you can make water do what you want it to do—to help you make things.

"Why didn't they tell us this when we were making ropes and when the girls were making baskets? Why didn't they teach us how to make them strong in our minds? You don't actually have to say it out loud. You can say it in your mind and you can think it and it will happen. That is what I heard."

A young girl spoke up. "When my granny wants things to be done I hear her ask for help. When she wants a skin to help her she speaks to it and asks it to help her. But how can we do that? How can we make a skin come alive? That is what I heard her saying, but I don't know what kind of skins she meant."

Shuyulh looked at the others and said, "Remember the skin that is soaking in front of the canoe?"

"Oh," one of them said. "Do you mean the grey whale skin?"

"Yes, the one we dragged down to the beach. The one we weighed down with rocks the girls had gathered so it wouldn't drift away."

Shuyulh's younger brother said, "Do you mean we can make it do what we want it to do?"

"That is what I learned while I was listening to the Elders," Shuyulh said. "That is what they do."

"How can they do that?"

The boys and girls talked for a long time and they came up with a plan: they would make a killer whale.

"During the night, we will go down to the beach and drag the skin around the point to this place," Shuyulh said. "The girls will be the look-outs."

One of the younger boys was worried. "It will take us all night," he said.

"Do they ever check on us when we sleep?" Shuyulh asked. "The only time they come is to wake us up. We will be all right as long as we are in bed when they come in the morning. We will bring the skin to our diving place and anchor it there until we use it."

Some of the girls were afraid because they thought the Elders would find out. Shuyulh said, "We will wait for a few days and we will go behind the bighouses where they have thrown away some of the spoiled wood. The wood is still good. The Elders have already spoken to those planks, so we won't have to talk to them much ourselves. We will get some of the rocks that have been spoken to and these rocks will weigh the skin down." One of the boys was directed to do this, since his grandfather was the one who speaks to the rocks.

Shuyulh said to the girls, "Your grandmothers talk to the ropes while they are making them. Get some of those ropes to tie the poles with. We need poles double our length so we can make the skin become a killer whale."

The children were scared but they were very excited as well.

One of the girls said, "I can see the grey whale skin from here. How are we going to make it into a killer whale?"

"That is where you come in," Shuyulh answered. "At night you will start taking some of the black paint and the white paint that is hidden under your mothers' beds. You will also get some from your aunties." Three of them had already learned to prepare paint so they knew what they were doing.

"Also, get as much tumulh as you can from the baskets under the platforms in the bighouse. We must have everything ready. We can't just take a little bit at a time or we won't be able to do it." Some of the younger ones were afraid and Shuyulh said, "If any of you are afraid, do not follow us but do not say anything to spoil our plan."

"Why are we doing this? Why are we making a killer whale?" one of the younger boys asked.

Shuyulh said, "How many of you have hidden in the evening or early morning just to listen to a little bit of the sacred lessons the Elders are giving to the older ones? If we do this and it becomes real then we will prove that we are like our older brothers and sisters."

"What if something happens?" one of the boys said.

"No, it will work," another one answered. "If we learn to do it the right way, then we will be just like our older brothers and sisters. The adults won't tell us to go away anymore."

"We aren't just children anymore," said Shuyulh, "and we have proven that by working. We will talk to the rocks and they will become part of us. We will talk to smuyuth (deer) and make the skin do what we want it to do. Nobody can do that unless they are knowledgeable. If we are thrown out of the village after we do this, we will go and make another village somewhere where we can use fish to do our work for us. We can use deer to run and be the watcher of our village. We can use mink to be our Elders because they know everything. Mink become like us some-times—like people—because they watch and listen to our old masters, our grandfathers. We can do that."

The young people crept back into the village and went to sleep. Early the next morning before the sun came up, the boys and girls did their chores. They brought in wood for the morning fire and water to make the herb teas and boil the dried fish.

One of the old ladies said, "Something is going on with these children. I can feel it."

"You are just getting old," her husband said. "All children become very active at this age. They don't listen to what we say anymore. They do what they want."

"This is different. I can feel it."

The children watched and waited and continued to help. They had signals now. Shuyulh taught them signals and body language. They could send a message by the way they threw their heads back and how they moved their eyes. One of them said, "I hear your voice telling me what to do even when you are not looking at me."

"It's good that you hear thoughts because that is what we will be doing when we are inside the skin," Shuyulh said.

The young people became so in tune with each other that each knew what the others were thinking at all times.

They gathered everything they needed and made all the preparations. One of the boys dug deep down in the sand to get old clamshells. The clamshells were ground up and used to make white paint. Only special clamshells could be used and only a few of the old ladies knew how to talk to them. The boys carried some of the fine split cedar, and while they were packing it, they talked to it and asked it to become light.

While they were working, they could feel the energy of the air and the trees. They said to the air and the trees, "Are you helping us? Do you feel sorry for us because we are being shunned by the others in the village?" Now they really felt they were being helped by the energies.

"I can feel them. I feel they are helping us," Shuyulh said. "They are going to help us do what we want them to do. The energy of the air, of Mother Earth, of the rocks, and of the trees will help us. The water is bubbling and yes, it will help us also." They were so excited now. "Tonight we will all go to the beach to start preparing. The older boys are going to help me. Some of the girls will have to stay home and listen. Who do you hear in your mind?" Shuyulh asked them. "Who do you talk to when they are not in sight?"

One of the girls said, "I talk to my cousin."

"Then your cousin will stay home and you will stand guard at our meeting place." Shuyulh asked the boys, "Who do you speak to when they are not in sight?"

One of the boys said, "I speak to my younger cousin."

"All right, he will stay home and you will send messages to each other." Everything was ready and they all had their partners.

"We will meet at the beach but we will call you one by one—we will contact you with our minds," Shuyulh said. "No torches will be used, but you will know where we are even in the dark. We will go when the tide is coming in. I have spoken to our grandfather qa'. The message I received is, 'We are waiting for you.' I've spoken to our grandfather the tide and asked him to put the little fish and the fluorescence in the water to sleep, so no one will know we are in the water."

That evening all the boys and girls gathered at their meeting place. Some went ahead to the hidden bay where they would take the skin. The others took the skin of the grey whale, qwunus, into the water. Some of the children were carrying the special rocks that they had left there. Some of them got underneath the skin, some of them got inside the skin, and some of them cut holes in the skin and laced the timbers through the holes. They talked to the skin constantly, pleading with it, praising it. And they could almost feel the skin swimming. When they were hungry, the children talked to themselves and they were no longer hungry, and when they were thirsty, they talked to themselves and they stopped being thirsty.

When the boys and girls went around the point, the tide started to change and the children quickened their pace. They were hurrying, hurrying. They pleaded with the skin to be safe so it would not be harmed or damaged. They spoke to the skin as if it were alive, saying, "If you are tired, we will stop," but the skin said, "No, keep going. I will help you." This made the children very happy. They were all listening to the skin now and understanding it. As they came around the rough and rocky point, they didn't even feel the rocks. It was almost as if they were walking on water.

The boys and girls reached the bay where the rest of the young people had made a little fire on the beach to guide the whale. As they saw it approach, they thanked the skin.

Everyone gathered together and ate some dried fish and deer meat and put some of the food underneath the skin to feed it. The skin was very happy. Then the young people weighed down the skin with the rocks. They remembered that they must speak to the four corners of the skin because of the four winds in the universe: north, south, east, and west. They talked to the winds as they worked, especially stuywut, the north wind. The children begged and pleaded with the wind to help them, as all the winds were their grandfathers. The west wind is tuṅcáluqw, meaning "lots of water." If you are lost at sea, the water will look after you. They pleaded with tuṅcáluqw to look after the skin.

As the young people spoke to the winds, they asked that the skin and the boys who would enter it become one. They asked tuṅwuq̓w, the east wind and the south wind, to support and help them with their power. The east wind is so far up in the mountains that they had to holler so their voices would reach this grandfather. When they were finished speaking to these winds they heard the eerie response, "Mmmmmmm."

Some of the children were afraid but Shuyulh said "hay ch q̓a', hay ch q̓a'" to the four winds.

Their work was done for the day and they snuck back home and slept until they heard the old ladies get up. Shuyulh woke his brother and said, "Our silu (grandmother) is up. We must get water for her."

The two boys weren't sleepy now because they knew they had a job to do. They grabbed the sk̓waw̓us (water baskets) and ran down to the water hole, filling the baskets as fast as they could. Then they went further out to the shoreline and jumped in the ocean. They knew they must not go to fresh water now. They must go to the salt water to honour it. They rubbed themselves with sand and then rubbed on the rocks. The rocks answered and said "hay ch q̓a'" to the boys for leaving some of their aroma on the rocks. The rocks would feed on this and become their helpers. Then they brought the water and firewood to their silu.

When they passed the enclosed area where some of the girls were sleeping, the boys called, "Are you awake? 'Umut (get up)." The girls got up and ran over to the next house to wake the other girls. They didn't have to go inside; they just went to the place where the girls slept and nodded and the girls woke up. The girls inside knew their cousins were telling them to get up.

Shuyulh and his brother sent a different kind of energy to the girls who lived on the edge of the village. These girls were sleeping in the woods because their families had disowned them and they were being punished. Although these girls were separated from their families, they always had enough food because they collected roots. The roots of the skunk cabbage and the roots of ferns were especially good when cooked.

When the boys had finished their chores, they asked their silu if they could have some dried fish and dried clams to take with them while they collected more wood in the hills. Their silu told them to take as much as they needed. Silu watched the boys and thought they didn't look the same anymore. When Shuyulh was leaving, he heard his silu saying that he looked so different that she must speak to his grandfather about starting to teach him because he was becoming a young man.

"Even his smell is different," she was thinking. "He smells like the fresh wood that is brought down from the hills, yet he also smells like very wet warm sand."

Shuyulh smiled to himself; he could hear what she was thinking.

"Yes, I can hear you also, my grandson," she said, surprising him. "Be happy this day, my grandson."

He was very happy now and he ran to join the others at their hiding place. The young people sat in a circle, not talking, but each one was praying. This is how they had been taught to pray. Each person prays in his or her own way, using their own energy first and then listening to others praying for them.

Once they were all together, Shuyulh prayed for everyone and told them what he had heard his grandmother say. "We must remember these words from her. She is sending us forth; she knows we are grown, that we are not children anymore. You girls are not children anymore; you are becoming women. If they do not accept you back in the village after this day, you must look after one another. When it is time for you to live with a man you must look for that person in another village—it must not be one of your relatives." He sounded like a little old man, like an ancient man who was dying.

"You are not going to die, are you?" one of the girls asked.

Shuyulh said, "I am going to live forever."

The boys and girls began their work. They laid out the long, "spoken-to" cedar sticks they had brought along. The longest one became the fin of q̓ullhánumucun, the killer whale. "This is the only way we are going to use this skin," Shuyulh said. "Our Elders have wanted a killer whale but no killer whale has come. Only qwunus, the grey whale, has come. We are going to stretch the skin on the rocks."

The rocks were honoured and said "hay ch q̓a'." The young people stretched the skin over the biggest rock and Shuyulh marked where the lines would be. He marked the top black, the bottom white, and the fins with little white tips. The sqe'eq (youngest boy) would be in the front holding the fire bag. The fire bag was used at other times to take fire with them when they journeyed far into the hills. Tonight they were going to use the fire bag to make smoke. When the whale surfaced they would blow smoke through the blowhole. They used the large kelp, cutting the bulb in half so it was like a funnel to take smoke from the fire pouch to the blowhole.

They talked to the kelp, pleading with it to honour them by becoming part of the blowhole. They knew that the kelp might not like the heat from the smoke, as it was not used to this. They explained, "It is very important that we have this smoke, which is part of our breath, to make the skin become alive with us in it."

The children had gathered black paint, white paint, and red ochre. "Why do we need the red ochre?" one of the younger girls asked.

"Red ochre represents blood," Shuyulh said. "Red ochre is a special gift from Mother Earth. It is very powerful."

The children had also collected q̓uyémun (clam-shells). The girls put their mouths on the clamshells to give them life, and then they put white markings along the blowhole and along the eyes with the white clamshells. The clamshells on the beach were making noises and a young clam said "Ssshhhhh," and they became quiet.

"This is our work, too," said the young clam. "All of you, all of us. We don't want the grandfathers and grandmothers to know we are here helping or we might get into trouble." Some of the clam Elders were very kind and willing to teach them, but some of them were mean and refused to help.

The girls were mixing the tumulh in great big clamshells. The clamshells said "oohhhhh" when they felt the red liquid in their pores and "hay ch q̓a'" when they were nourished by the tumulh. They had been buried for so long and now they were dripping red ochre from the bottom of their porous shells and their little tongues were licking it up. The girls were laughing and petting the little clamshells.

Then the girls and boys crawled inside the skin to paint it with the red ochre, and it went into all the crevices. The skin lapped it up, making appreciative noises. Some of the boys were painting red ochre on the long sticks, saying, "Breathe, my little brothers and my big brothers." The sticks ate it up and became pliable, loving it.

The girls took long ropes made from stinging nettle to sew the skin together. The skin said, "I am going to be whole again. I am going to be me again."

Everyone was very excited. It was almost like the skin was blowing up as they moved it; it was like a huge bubble on the beach. The skin was buoyant and floating. They were putting the long sticks inside to become the ribs and pushing the clamshells and sticks into the tail. Then they squeezed a very small boy into the tail and he giggled and giggled. Next they pushed the smallest boy into the nose, as it wasn't a very long nose.

The mouth was very big; it took its shape from the bodies of several young boys. One boy crouched down inside; he was the holder of the fire. They inserted the q̓uyém̓un into the eye sockets, making the whale's white eyes. Next to the little one who was the fire holder was another short boy who would steer the skin. The oldest boy, Shuyulh, held the longest pole, now the whale's fin.

The skin had become q̓ullhánumucun, the killer whale. The boys inside the skin were painted with red ochre. They asked their bodies to become the body and the flesh of the whale. The girls made little holes on the bottom of the skin for the boys' feet. They lined up special rocks along the belly of the whale— rocks painted with red ochre and white paint. Now everyone was in place. The firekeeper was in his place, the one who moved the eyes was crouched inside, the small one inside the tail was ready, and all those in the middle section were ready.

The girls started to sew the belly closed. Everything was covered in red ochre. They started to blow inside the skin and the skin started to fill out.

The boys inside the whale skin were moving in the water now. The children on the beach were *ohhhh*-ing and *ahhhhh*-ing as they looked at it. It actually looked like q̓ullhánumucun—the one that didn't come around anymore. Some of them were scared and yet they were also excited and happy. They knew they must be happy for the whale before it would work, and they knew that it heard them. The whale said, "I am here, I am with you," as the children pushed it into the ocean.

The whale went out into the ocean and then it dove down. When it came up to the surface, it was shiny and wet and it blew smoke out with water, just like real whales do. It started to swim towards the point. The girls and boys started to run along the point, hollering and encouraging the whale and praising it. They ran to the village hollering, "There is a great whale out there. It is the killer whale, q̓ullhánumucun, not qwunus."

Grandfather wanted a killer whale for its skin, but he didn't bother to look because the children were always lying. One of the women looked up and said, "There is a funny-looking whale out there. It *is* the one that rarely comes our way."

The boys inside the skin stayed close to shore so their feet could run on the sand but then one of the little boys said, "My feet are inside. The skin is moving by itself. It is swimming on its own!"

The boys just wanted to show the village that they were there, to show the adults what they could do.

They didn't want this to happen, for the skin to swim by itself, out of their control. They asked the skin to help them, but they received no answer.

The old grandfather went down to the shore, running slowly, since he was very old. Some young fellows ran alongside him, held him underneath his arms, and ran with him, in the way it was done long ago. Grandfather called the whale to come close. He said, "It is going away—it is going out to sea. Get your canoes and spears. I want that whale." The young men went to a special canoe that was already loaded; everything was ready in the canoe. They even had water and food in the canoe in case the whale took them out to sea.

By this time, Shuyulh knew they were becoming one with the whale. He said to his brother, "See if you can move."

His brother said, "I can't move on my own. It is like I am part of you now." The firekeeper also knew he was no longer blowing the smoke, yet every time the whale surfaced the smoke blew out on its own.

The boy who was steering said, "The whale is telling me to hang on. It is telling me there is a canoe coming our way and the spearsmen are standing up.

Can you see them? No? But the eyes are telling me. I can see through the eyes. Our uncle is there and our father is holding a spear."

"This cannot be," Shuyulh said. "Get close to shore."

"I can't! I can't seem to push the skin close to shore! I can't feel my feet! I can't feel the rocks beneath my feet!"

Shuyulh said to the skin, "My brothers are becoming afraid. Please release us and let us drop to the sand."

"It cannot be done," the whale said. "We are one now. Each one of you has become one with me."

They were all thinking to themselves, "We are one. We are one."

By this time the grandfather was at the water's edge and he heard the sound of Xeel's, the Creator in the heavens. Many of the others heard the voice of Xeel's as well.

"You have forgotten the teachings of the old ways. You must teach the children as they grow. You must start teaching them when they first start to walk and continue teaching them as they grow. Do not neglect the teachings." The Creator was very sad, because he felt it was too late.

Now the grandfather was yelling at the men with spears. "Stop! There is something wrong with that whale. The whale—it is not what it seems to be." But it was too late. The spear spiraled in the air for a long time and then went straight for the whale.

The firekeeper yelled, "My brother has a spear in him. And we are receiving messages from outside, from our grandfather."

They all heard it. The grandfather knelt down by the water's edge and put his head right in the water. The young men were trying to hold him back, but the old ladies told the boys to let him be.

"He can't communicate if you touch him. He has to have his own energy. He knows what he is doing."

Grandfather was in the water, with his head underwater. They were afraid he would drown but he was speaking in the water.

"Are you my grandsons?"

"Yes, we are, Grandfather," Shuyulh said. "We are your grandsons but we are now one with the whale. I am now one with my younger brothers and my younger cousins. We have become one with my brother in the tail and we have all become the head and the brain as well. One of our brothers is dead but he is still alive inside of us. He has a spear in him; somebody is pulling the spear out now."

The grandfather said, "It is the energy of the water. You are one with the water now."

"Grandfather, we are very sorry for what we have done," Shuyulh said. "We were angry that you didn't want to share the sacred teachings with us. We heard some of the teachings but we didn't know the right words or the right way to do it, and this is what happened to us. We used the skin of qwunus to become q̓ullhánumucun, the killer whale."

The grandfather was crying now. He surfaced and told his older grandsons—the ones who had received the teachings—what had happened.

"Tell them we are very sorry for shunning them and chasing them away," the older grandsons said.

"It is our fault. It is my fault," the grandfather said. "I will carry this into the next world. The next generations will know better. The teachings will go on but in a different way. There will be fewer teachings for the younger ones, but the teachings will increase as the young ones grow. Nothing will be held back. In this way our people will live a long time and in harmony."

Then the grandfather spoke directly to those who had become the whale. "Forgive us and forgive me, my children. We want to thank you for the teachings you have given us. How else would we have known what words can do to make a skin come alive again? But sacrificing yourselves is a very hard and sorrowful way to find out. We will call the other children, we will heal them, and we will work with them in their healing, remembering the loss of you."

The grandfather paused a moment, then said, "I can see in my mind that there is a whale pod around the point. Go join them. I am asking them to honour you and accept you. I am asking them not to be afraid of the smell of qwunus on your skin. But perhaps by the time you reach there the aroma of qwunus will have changed into the aroma of q̓ullhánumucun, the killer whale."

By this time the spear was out of the whale and it was drifting away. Shuyulh's father picked up the spear as they stood and waved and sang a mournful song to the young men who had become a killer whale. He said, "This will be an honoured place. Even after I am gone it will still be a place of honour, and we will honour the lives of all killer whales. They are our brothers, fathers, grandfathers, healers, and educators in the ways of the water."

The people began to walk back to the village and the old man sent forth the fathers and mothers of the children banished to the woods and told them to bring the children home. Grandfather said, "We have a lot of healing to do."

Speaking with Ellen about "The Boys Who Became a Killer Whale"

THIS IS A story of alienated youth, about young people just entering puberty who feel angry and rebellious. They are trying to prove their independence and worth, and at the same time they are questioning authority. The story shows how young people can suffer harsh consequences because of their behaviour. The adults and Elders in the story learn a hard lesson, too, about their responsibilities to their children's education. They come to realize that their role in training their children is vital and that they must not neglect it. They also realize that the *way* you teach a child can be just as important as *what* you teach a child. It is still true today that young people must learn the basic skills of daily living before they proceed to more advanced teachings. The story reminds us that teaching basic life skills is vital to the survival of humankind and that spiritual teachings must not be forgotten.

The story begins with a group of young people, angry at the adults of their community who treated them like babies, or so they thought. They were eager to know all the teachings, but they were not included at teaching time. Their cousins and siblings weren't much older, yet they were included. When they wanted to help, or to remedy a difficult situation they may have caused, they were not given explanations but were yelled at and told to go away. So now they were determined to make their own decisions and plans so they could prove their worth to the community.

These young people didn't understand that the community was following a set path for their training, and that they needed to pass through each stage of development in the proper order. They were impatient, leaping ahead, thinking of what more they could learn. They felt they had been at their present stage for many winters and many summers, and they had had enough.

The adults in the story did not understand the importance of setting the stage for learning and creating a positive learning environment. For example, one important lesson the young people felt they were missing out on was how to "speak to the rope" and "honour the rope" so that it would not break. Their thirst for knowledge was clear, but they found it difficult to approach the adults with their questions—and the adults were not helping the situation by becoming angry and refusing to explain.

The adults were missing an opportunity to perhaps lay the young people's concerns to rest. They could have given a brief explanation in order to lay the groundwork for future teachings, such as giving a very basic lesson about "speaking to" objects and "honouring" objects. This opening might also have allowed them to introduce the idea of learning certain things first before they move on to the next ones, and to reassure the young people that all the teachings would come to them in good time.

Xeel's teaches the importance of respecting all things, both living and non-living. The people were taught to "speak to" the tree and honour it if they were going to take bark from it or cut it down to make a canoe. Animate and inanimate things exist together in the universal energy and support each other. The importance of this belief was shown in the story by the use of tumulh (red ochre), which comes from deep within Mother Earth. It is taught that when water hits certain kinds of dirt or minerals, it becomes different in substance, "two in one," or maybe more than two. Tumulh was used so much because it united many different forms of energy into one.

From the story we learn that we must have a conscious connection to the objects we are asking to help us—the tree, bark, and water—and that we must believe that they will help us. Perhaps this is how we get our energy. The children knew from listening to their grandparents that it was possible to communicate with inanimate objects. Some of the children overheard the Elders talking about qa' (water) and about how you can make it do what you want it to do by just saying it in your mind. However, the young people were missing some of the teaching. When the topic of the whale skin came up, they knew it was possible to make skins come alive, but they didn't ask themselves whether they should first understand the whole teaching. Because they felt shunned and neglected whenever they asked to learn something new, they were determined not to go to the adults for guidance.

Does this sound familiar to you? In today's world, just as in the story, if you are taught in an angry way, your whole being remembers this. The teaching remains inside of you in an angry state, and it will come out of you in an angry way. The anger will show in the outer energy of your body. Even if other lessons are given in a kind voice, the memory of the angry voice is still there and it discourages you from approaching the adults to ask for help.

The young people had not realized how many things they had learned very well, as they showed when they made their preparations. They were knowledgeable enough to gather only materials that had been "spoken to." They gathered tumulh, and it is significant that they were aware of its importance. As Shuyulh said in the story, red ochre represents blood and is a special gift from Mother Earth. From the lessons they had learned, the children also knew about signals, body language, and communicating with their minds. They had practiced this skill and were able to communicate with each other when they were inside the skin. They also knew about the energy of the air, trees, rocks, and earth. They thought they hadn't learned anything, but still they knew what to do.

They gave food to the skin of the grey whale to nourish it. The skin had become alive in the minds of the young people. It was happy and the children were happy. When both sides are happy and working together, the way is paved for the work to be joyous, to be easy, and to take on a life of its own.

Have you had this experience of joyous work with others? If we approach a project with good thoughts, and we nourish an idea and send good energy to it, it will turn out differently than if we go into it with negative, unhappy thoughts. When we plan an event such as a wedding, a potlatch, or a family gathering, each person must know what he or she is going to be doing. Every event takes preparation, planning, and prayer. If an event is planned in a positive way and the feelings are light and happy, the event will flow well. People will not go away feeling depressed or harmed by it. In our daily lives, too, we must think about what we are doing and how we are going to do it. In order to be successful in life we must remember to prepare for the day, plan for the day, and pray to ask what we can bring forth to help us in our day.

The children remembered to pray to Xeel's, to acknowledge the four winds of the universe and to continue talking to the whale skin as they worked. We can think of the different types of wind as messengers from the universe representing movement and change. A certain wind tells us spring is coming, foretelling that all things in nature will come alive, helping the first buds on the trees come alive. Stuywut, the north wind, comes early in the spring to open the eyes of the trees so they will look at the world and spread their pollen, ensuring the continuation of the species. The west wind is called tuṅcáluqw, which means "lots of water." This is important for the salmon, showing them when it is time to start finding their way to their river. In fall, the trees offer a part of themselves to eat; the winds come to break off the leaves, and Mother Earth eats the leaves. Fall is the time to thank Mother Earth, and then rest for the winter. Nature recycles and builds upon itself. Tuṅwuq̓w, the east wind and south wind, tell us when the cold weather is awakening to cover us with new energy. The south wind helps the sun to move and shift against the north wind. Just like everything in nature, we need new energy four times a year. The trees need a time to recycle, the fish a time to go up the river, and the birds a time to lay their eggs.

Cultures around the world recognize the lessons of the four winds and the four seasons. The number four in our culture is significant as it represents the elements fire, water, air, and earth. There is significance in the four posts of the bighouse and the four limbs of our body that provide support as we reach out to the energy of the universe. We walk barefoot on Mother Earth to connect to earth energy and raise our arms to the sky, to Xeel's.

The children in the story talked to the winds of the universe and they did not forget to pray, sitting in a circle, each person praying in their own way, with their own energy, and then praying as a group. They remembered to speak to the skin and everything else that was there to help—the rocks, kelp, clamshells, and sticks. They praised all of these items and remembered to honour them in a respectful way. Some of the boys were painting red ochre on long sticks and telling the sticks to breathe. The sticks ate up the ochre and became pliable, loving it.

The momentum of their idea was building, and as it built it moved into another dimension of reality. There is the "thought" before the "thought." This is the thought before doing, the point of transformation in thought that leads to manifestation. Can we use this technique in today's world? Yes, we can—we just need to be aware that this can happen.

The children wanted to prove themselves to the village by transforming the grey whale skin into a living killer whale. Once the boys were inside the whale skin and were painted with red ochre, all their energy was focused on asking their bodies to become one with the whale skin so they could then transform into the body and the flesh of their killer whale, q̓ullhánumucun. They had intended all along to do this, but at the moment of transformation they became afraid because they were no longer in control.

In today's world, young people sometimes face similar situations in which they set out in anger and rebellion to prove themselves, but then lose control and become fearful. They travel into unknown territory, then don't know how to get out of the situation.

The children in the story wanted to show the village that they could appear as a whale and accomplish something great without the help of the Elders. They hadn't thought about the consequences of their actions, and now they were under attack by the hunters. The whale faced an unexpected tragedy. The children had not considered what might go wrong if they weren't fully trained in the spiritual world. Spiritual knowledge takes years to master, and only people trained by their Elders can carry out spiritual work. It is not for the novice or for those who have bits and pieces of knowledge. Otherwise dire consequences might have to be faced.

The importance of the necessary forethought, training, and knowledge is emphasized in this story. This is a story which is useful to all ages but especially to those in pursuit of spiritual teachings. The energies of the universe can be powerful and potent enemies as well as allies. We must respect the fact that inanimate objects as well as animate ones can be used in a spiritual way.

This is illustrated at the end of the story when the grandfather put his head in the water and was able to communicate through it. He had known there was something wrong; he could feel it. He was listening to himself, to his inner knowing that comes from Xeel's, the Creator. It was telling him there was something wrong even though to all appearances he was seeing a normal killer whale. How often in our lives do we know that something doesn't look right, but we choose to ignore the message? The more we ignore these messages, the less they will come to us.

At the moment of transformation—of becoming one—the grandsons were with the grandfather. This was also the moment when the whale was speared, a climactic moment of life and death, death and rebirth, for in death there is a new beginning. The grandsons were now able to share with their grandfather their regret, sorrow, and anger for what they had done. They were able to acknowledge that their lack of spiritual training had brought a horrible end to the life they had known. This tragic moment also gave their people a lesson never to be forgotten.

One of the teachings in our culture is that killer whales are not edible. A person who eats a killer whale can acquire that sort of mind and become mean. This story was told to teach young and old alike what it means to pass on knowledge in a kind and caring way, not in a mean and harmful way. We can pass on to the next generation a way of thinking and a way of being. If we are always making mistakes and we continue on this path, can we be the cause of problems for the next generation? Does it just become a way of behaving without any thought of how we can change? We can teach our minds very easily if we have the desire. It is vital to pass on our teachings to future generations, but we must be aware of what we are teaching and how we are doing it.

In today's world, the lessons children need to learn may be a bit different, but it is still true that children do not learn unless we teach them. If children are told before they enter a new situation what to expect and what is expected of them, they are more comfortable and will know how to behave. When you do this you are setting guidelines for a child to follow. Start with basic teachings and explain that there is a time for eating, a time for playing, a time for rest, a time for stories, a time for lessons, and so on—and that the teachings will progress over time. It is important to tell children why they are learning whatever they are learning to do, and to let them know that the teachings will continue. In this way they won't rebel or get angry if teachings are thrust upon them suddenly or sporadically.

As children grow older, there will be other lessons to pass on, such as respect for other cultures. Children will not learn to appreciate the differences in cultures if we don't talk about them. An important lesson is the appreciation of other nationalities, their cultures and spiritual ways of life. An understanding of life and its differences helps children see the world from a new perspective. They begin to understand that their way is not the only way. It is not the only truth.

Another valuable teaching that comes from this story is the honouring of the killer whale for all time. We are taught to respect the killer whale, who gives us support while we are in the water. Killer whales are our fathers, grandfathers, brothers, healers, and educators in the ways of the water. This teaching has been passed on from generation to generation. It is understood that all things are related and we must all look after one another. It has never been more important than it is now to remember this, as we see our animal brothers and sisters disappearing from Mother Earth.

At the end of the story, the significance of what had happened to the boys who became a whale was recognized, and it moved the community into action. They headed back to the village, and the grandfather sent forth the fathers and mothers of the children banished to the woods to bring them home so the community could get on with the healing that was needed.

The story ends with the grandfather saying to the people, "We have a lot of healing to do." These words hold significance for us today. There are so many social problems such as homeless children, alcohol and drug abuse, bullying, suicide, and many more. So many young people are becoming lost or, as the story puts it, "banished to the woods." We need to go and look for them, be with them, talk with them, teach them. If we feel at a loss about how to do this, perhaps we can reach out to others who can help us.

We are at a point in history where we must look at what is taking place within our families. Are we teaching our young people what they need to know in order to survive and thrive? Are we teaching them basic life skills and spiritual skills that will sustain them through hard times? Are we teaching them in a consistent and caring way so they will want to learn from us and will come to us when they have a problem?

Talking to children when they are very young and telling them what to expect in each situation helps open the lines of communication. If the lessons are given in a compassionate way from the beginning of a child's life, the child is open and receptive. This paves the way for future teachings and communication.

Young people may still become angry and rebellious and create a situation in which they may harm themselves and those around them. Unfortunately, some of these young people become lost souls. Perhaps this is the time when the fathers and mothers of the children who have been "banished to the woods" bring the children home and spend the time to heal with them.

The Sockeye That Became a Rainbow

A LONG TIME ago when the world was first created, Xeel's, the Creator roamed the earth teaching the animals, his first creations. Xeel's said that people and animals must live together, play together, and share food together now and then.

Xeel's knew that the time of summer was coming to an end. He decided that the people of the sea should visit one another before some of them journeyed up the river to renew themselves. The sockeye salmon, spring salmon, coho salmon, and dog salmon were all destined to journey up the river.

But there were others who did not make this journey. The Creator said to the salmon, "You must say goodbye to your relatives from the deep." So the fish from the deep were called, the codfish and red snapper.

The first ones to come to shore were the sockeye salmon. These were the most beautiful of the salmon family with different colours shimmering on their skin: red like the sun, yellow like the moon, and blue like the ocean. When they disrobed they took off their masks first and then their outer garments. They were sure to fold the outsides of their garments inwards so they wouldn't dry out.

The Creator said, "Cover your masks so the energy on them won't be shared with others. It is very important to have guards of your own, so four of your Elders will sit with the robes."

The Elders sat on the beach guarding the garments so that others did not touch them, and they kept the garments moist at all times. They kept children away from the area to protect the garments from them. It was the job of the older women of the clan to remind the young ones that this was necessary, since the young ones might forget. The Creator said to the old ladies of the clan, "Keep talking to the young ones, and keep reminding them how sacred their garments are."

Next came the big spring salmon.

"Those are your big brothers and big sisters," the Creator said.

They were very heavy on top but their legs were not very long. They sometimes tripped when they were playing and the other salmon would laugh at them. The springs would take some of the scales from their skin and throw them at the others.

"Don't waste your scales like that," the Creator said. "The rocks like it when you swim over them because your scales tickle them. You need your scales." Now there were many fish on the beach.

Next came the coho, who were smaller and very sleek and beautiful. The coho talked a lot and now they were talking amongst themselves in whispering voices. The Creator tried to listen to what they were saying. Xeel's heard that the coho were afraid of the others and they hesitated before removing their garments.

Xeel's whispered to them since he didn't want the others to hear. "You are all related. Never be afraid of one another. You even have the same body aroma. Sniff. Can you smell one another?"

They were afraid to answer loudly to the Creator so they just nodded, still whispering and laughing. Xeel's thought to himself, "These are the cheeky ones." He smiled deeply within himself and thought, "They know what I am thinking. I have taught them well."

Suddenly Xeel's became very happy and excited, and he said, "They are here." The fish on the beach didn't have to ask. They knew. "Your Elders are here, the k̓waluxw, the dog salmon. These are the great ones, your grandfathers and grandmothers. These are the Elders of our future—the sacred ones who will pave the way for all of you to carry the lessons from the past into the future so you will never lose your way. It will be written in the rocks."

When the dog salmon marched up the beach, even the water recoiled and the sound came, "Oooowwwww."

The older ones left their slime behind as they travelled up the beach. This made it easy for the younger ones to follow them. The pebbles and sand also appreciated the slime left behind, and said "hay ch q̓aʼ." When the dog salmon removed their garments they made a lot of noise, because their outer garments were so thick.

The Creator reminded them to pile their garments closely together instead of folding them individually. The Creator said, "You have a lot of slime on you—this is your lifeline. This is your connection. It will draw you back to where you are from. If you fold your garments by themselves you will not be able to open them when you put them back on."

Their inner bodies were so tough looking and so shiny. The other salmon watched from a distance and said, "They even have slime inside their skin." They looked at their own bodies and said, "Do we have that? Are we shiny like them?"

The Creator knew what they were saying and he said to all the fish people, "You are not all exactly alike, yet you are brothers and sisters. You had to be different."

Xeel's continued to advise the salmon people. "You will journey up the river before the snow comes. You will not return in body, but you will have many descendants who will replace you. Your physical presence will be replaced by memory—the memory of the ocean and of the fresh water rivers which you have inherited from previous generations and which you have been carrying through your life. Through your descendants, your memories will be carried into the future. The generations who come after you will honour you, because the memories will be there for them to know and honour."

While the Creator was speaking, all the fish people were saying, "Aahhhhhhh, aahhhhhhh." Even though their arms were short, they had their arms raised to the sky to say hay ch q̓a'.

The Creator told them, "You will be able to connect with one another's minds. You will know what each other is thinking."

Then Xeel's hollered, "They are coming, they are coming. The ones from the deep are coming."

Those already gathered were so excited that their relatives from the deep were arriving. The water turned red as they floated to the surface. They were already walking before they hit the shore. Their outer garments were bright red and everyone went "ooohhhhh." The children wanted to run down to the shore to greet them and the old ladies said, "Don't you touch them. You might still have some slime on your fingers and you might hurt yourself. Their scales are very hard and tough since they need this protection when they are in xwt̓lup (the deep)."

Coming were the tuqwtuqw, the red snappers. The eldest red snapper came first as they marched up the beach, then the young men so proud, so beautiful. The tuqwtuqw children were told to be careful when folding their skins so they wouldn't dry out. The Creator told them to look after their garments. He knew they were listening, since they said "ahhhhhh," and they looked at one another and nodded. They knew what to do. They lined up their garments properly on the beach and the garments were shiny, beautiful and red. They knew if they laid their garments out properly they wouldn't float away when the water rose.

The red snappers were so proud when they disrobed. They took a long time to do so. They loved to prance around for everyone to see their beautiful skin under their outer garments. Everyone present said, "ohhhhhhhhh."

The children of the salmon family asked nucím (why) they weren't red inside just like the outside. The Creator heard them and lifted his finger to say "shhhh." The children listened to Xeel's and paid attention to the proceedings.

Next came the thaaq (big heads). These were the łq̓as, the rock cod. They always made funny noises when they walked, "ooomommpooomommp." They walked up the beach very slowly and took long breaths before they disrobed. They were taking in the new air and they remembered to thank their life-giver, the salt water.

The cod grandmothers always had their mouths puckered up and if their mouths weren't puckered up, the cod people would look at one another and worry. When their mouths were puckered, everyone was happy.

One of the grannies had her arms raised to the sky, thanking everyone on the beach. She said, "Aaʼ siːʼém̓ nu siyéy̓u (Oh, my dear relatives), I am so glad you are all here. We always come last because we can't stay out of the water for very long. Even though we are different, we are still alike in our thinking and in our appreciation for the one who sits up on that rock, the one who guides us, and we truly thank him."

They all lifted their arms to Xeel's where he sat. The old people coached the children not to think evil, because Xeel's always knew every thought. The children thought, "How could he know what we are thinking? There are so many of us." They looked down to the beach. They knew Xeel's was looking at them with a knowing smile on his face.

The Creator would look around into the surrounding areas and nod, thanking those who came to watch but not join the festivities. These were the little mice, the snakes, a raccoon, a deer, the mink, an otter, the elk, and a bear. When he looked up to the woods and nodded, the fish standing on the beach looked up and raised their arms to the sky and nodded, too. They knew the animal people were there. They were not alone. They felt protected.

Now that they were all gathered, they noticed that fires were going in the corners of the field. They didn't question the Creator about who made the fires. The fires were warm. They didn't want to go near them or touch them.

There were sticks in the field and big balls made out of pitch from the trees. The trees gave the pitch freely, saying, "Remember, these people don't want to be sticky so be very careful. We will only throw the round soft balls onto the field."

The boys and girls all played together while the Elders sat on the logs surrounding the field. The Elders gave thanks to the logs, since the Creator had put them there. The children followed their Elders' lead and gave thanks and appreciation for the balls, sticks, and the baskets in the four corners. The girls were always afraid to run to the four corners for fear of the relatives they had only glimpsed. The elk had fire coming out of their eyes, as this is just the way they are, but they were also enjoying the festivities on the field. In the darkest corner, the girls could see the huge mask of the bear and they wondered what he would look like if he removed his mask. They wondered if he *could* remove his mask!

Xeel's said, "That you will never know, because they are a different species. They will remove their masks at their own special time, but not amongst you. The breath of their body is different than yours, their energy is also different, but they are your relatives. That is all you may know for now."

As evening came, the Creator pointed with his long stick to a large basket at the foot of the rock he sat on. He said, "Come, my children. Nourish yourself with these gifts. This food is the welcoming, strengthening life-giver. This food will sustain you while you are away from your home."

They all said, "Ahhhh. Hay ch q̓a'. Hay ch q̓a', Men (Father)."

The baskets were filled with berries that were all different. They didn't question where they came from even though they knew it was not the time of year for salmonberries, huckleberries, or salal berries. They just loved the berries because they were small enough for them to eat and they were very delicate. They would take just one and suck the juice out of it. The juice ran down the chins of the little ones and the older ones would lick their skin to get the juice off. Always, they remembered to say "hay ch q̓a'."

When evening came, they all lined up, each with their own people. They knew which line they belonged to. The Creator sat and watched as his children prepared to return to the ocean. They marched down the beach and put on their garments.

They were very careful when they put on their masks, lifting them to the four directions: north, south, east, and west. They followed one another down the beach, all the while nodding and waving at the Creator. When the last group passed, there was one girl who kept looking back. Her name was Tl'useep.

The Creator wondered what she was looking for since her people were already in the water. Then the Creator saw one young man from the sockeye people still on shore.

When everyone had left, the water sent a huge wave to wash the beach and everything was just as it had been before the gathering. The water cleansed the beach and the slime on the beach was gone. The water stood up and thanked Xeel's for the day. The Creator waved his arm across the landscape and the baskets and the berries were gone. The field was just as it was—no balls, no sticks, no baskets. He stood on the rock and waved his staff towards the woods and thanked the animals that lingered there.

The next morning before the sun rose over the horizon, the Creator was already sitting on the rock. He lifted his arms to praise Grandfather Sun. Xeel's said, "With your warmth, look after all the things that you have helped to put on this earth. This place is their home now and forever, and we must make certain they are looked after. The creatures of the water are not able to look after themselves when they are not in their own element, so we must do that for them. In the future, whoever comes to watch them gather must watch from a distance and not think any evil of these people who disrobe and join one another. We also thank the salt water who gives them life, who lets them carry the breath of the water so they will be able to breathe on land." The Creator thanked the Sun for his help.

The new day was just like the day before had been. The rainbow people, the sockeye, came again. They liked to turn their bodies to show them off. They were not red yet but you could see their bodies were sleek and colourful and the animals watching from the woods went "Mmmmmmm." When the sockeye disrobed, they were very careful with their masks. They took their masks off and blew into them because they still wanted to be connected. It was the same as the preceding day.

Next came the big spring salmon, the beautiful sleek coho, and then came the biggest ones, the dog salmon. It was too early for the dog salmon, yet they had to join the group. They were called the earth people because they had walked on earth before. They couldn't walk properly on earth, so they had to return to the water. The red snappers came next and lastly the codfish. They all disrobed and went up into the field to greet one another.

They were so happy to see one another again and this time they were comfortable touching each other's hands. The Elders now allowed them to do this. When they had gone back into the water the previous night, the Elders had touched the young ones and smelled them to see if they carried any body smell of the others. The Elders were very proud to say, "We know how to protect ourselves so we don't take the aroma from others."

The field was just the same as it had been the day before. The Creator pointed, and all of a sudden there were baskets, the sticks were there to be used as tools to push the pitch balls around, and the basket of berries was also there. The Sun was so kind. He wouldn't open his eyes for fear of drying the bodies. The old ladies watched the activities and they always guarded the young men and young women. The old ladies of the sockeye were masters at preparing the food so delicately. They mixed the berries with the weeds from the water and fed the people. Another day had come to an end.

That evening, one of the grandfathers said to his wife, "You must watch our eldest grandson. Tomorrow you must sit and watch."

The next day when they gathered, the people were very tense. They didn't play too much since this was their last day together.

At midday, the sockeye grandfather called his grandson to sit with him and his grandmother. He said, "You have been holding hands with one of the other species, the cod girl. You have been together for the last two days. I know which garment she belongs to, and this must not happen today. Do not hold her hand today. I do not want you to be with her today."

The young man said, "She is not so different from us. She is no different from me, only she wears a different garment."

The old man said, "She cannot join us and I will tell you why. She belongs to the deep, to the rock people; we belong to the river up in the mountains where we go to become many. We are not going to come back from there. You cannot bring her with you."

That day the old lady followed the young man along the trails to watch him. When they were ready to depart, there was a lot of sadness, especially for these two young ones. The old man and the old lady of the sockeye looked at one another as the young girl Tl'useep donned the ugliest of the masks. She belonged to the grey people with the big teeth and the big gills that were not to be used in fresh water. She would die if she entered fresh water. The young man cried as he sat on the beach waiting for his turn to go into the water.

The Creator watched from a distance and he knew. Then he said to the sockeye people, as he had spoken to them before, "You must go now and change your bodies, and through your offspring you will become many. You will not be here in body, but your memories will always be present. Even though your descendants will be different, the memories of your journey will always remain. And the pain of your sacrifice for future generations will always be there, so you must deal with it now before you make your last journey up the river to the spawning grounds."

They all waved and then they slipped into the water. The young man surfaced many times and the old lady and old man stayed close but he kept surfacing. He went behind a rock and stayed there for a while and the old man said, "He is communicating with her."

The old lady said, "Yes, he is able to penetrate through the salt water and the shell of the tough mask."

When evening came, the sockeye family was at the second falls, getting ready to go to the third falls. The water was not very high so they stayed there. The young man jumped onto the rocks and stayed there for the longest time crying. His Elders and the Creator were concerned for him.

The Creator said to him, "Would you be willing to join me up here to watch over your species?"

He didn't know what the Creator meant but he said, "I don't want to go up the river and change. I don't want to leave Tl'useep. I want to stay here."

Once he said this he came right out of the water with such a force that he shed his skin. All of a sudden there he was, a big blob on the rock, beautiful shining, shimmering colours, brilliant colours.

The Creator said to him, "You could be useful way up there in the sky. I will stretch you and you will be called thuqulshúnum, the rainbow. You will help me to bring in the waters. When you cry, the rains will come and the ponds of water where your family wait will be filled, and they will be able to reach the falls to jump up them. They will not be heavy now, as they are only souls."

"I will do it," the young man said. "I want to do it, but I still want her—I want Tl'useep."

The Creator said, "I will help you to bring her up to you. After you have been there for one night your body will be accepted, and then you will be able to stretch Tl'useep up to the sky so she will be close to you."

The young man became very happy that he would be able to have Tl'useep with him. The Creator grabbed him and threw him up and stretched him across the sky and there was the beautiful thuqulshúnum̓: red, green, yellow, blue. He felt himself shivering and quivering and he did that until the next day and then he was totally whole and accepted. He thanked the "no air" as he was now in "no air" country.

The next night he sang a sad mournful song, "*Tl'useepee-ye, Tl'useepee-ye*. Where are you?"

She sang back, "*Eetsun aw ee, Eetsun aw ee,* I am here."

They called to each other. It sounded so pitiful, so sad, so full of tears and pain. He cried, and then she cried, and the rains came and the thunder came. He could see the rivers and the ponds getting bigger and bigger, and his relatives started to jump up into the third falls, and they were aiming for the fourth falls. Now he remembered what the Creator had said, to stretch his arms out, grab Tl'useep, and stretch her to the sky.

Xeel's said, "I cannot do this for you since she is for you."

Tl'useep hadn't gone into the deep with her family, for she knew he would come for her. She sat on a rock waiting for him.

He thanked the Creator in his mind. "Thank you, Father, thank you." His arms went out and he sang his song again, "*Tl'useepee'ye, Tl'useepee'ye.* Where are you? I am waiting for you. Here is my hand. Take my hand."

Then he saw her reach out to him. He saw her hand, then he felt it, and he was so happy inside. He knew the Creator was guiding him. He felt her fingertips and her hand and he remembered the feeling of holding her. The memory of her was still there. With that thought in his mind, he pulled her hand, and he heard a huge crack in the rock and she came away from it. He could see her floating and he pulled and pulled as hard as he could. There was another big crack and suddenly she was glued under him. He remembered the Creator saying, "The slime from your bodies will mingle together and become one."

When they touched one another, it was just like they were floating in water. Their tears were mingling. Then the rain and the thunder came again. He could see that his family was able to swim easily up the river to the spawning grounds to become renewed.

He said, "Hay ch q̓aʼ, Xeelʼs, the Father, and hay ch q̓aʼ to the four winds." He knew that each one of the female salmon would have many, many offspring, each of whom would carry the memories of the past generations. In the new life cycle, the little ones thanked and caressed the older ones, who dissolved into the water and the pebbles. The pebbles and sand were hungry and devoured the old ones and thanked them, as it had been a long, long time since they had tasted such beautiful morsels of food. They said, "Mmmmmmmm. Hay ch q̓aʼ siˑʼém̓. Thank you to our many, many relatives. See you again next year."

Speaking with Ellen about
"The Sockeye That Became a Rainbow"

THIS IS A creation story explaining how the rainbow came to be, but it goes much deeper into an understanding of ourselves and our world by focusing on relationships. Xeel's, the Creator calls all the fishes of the sea to a great gathering on the shore. As the salmon and the deep-sea fish mingle, we witness various types of relationships, those between different species of fish, between Elders and children, between the animate and inanimate worlds—and between Xeel's, the Creator and his creations. We also see the special relationship between two people that we call love.

The story makes us think of our relationship with ourselves, other people, the environment, and even our past. In each case, the teachings of Xeel's guide the way we behave. Respect is emphasized above all: respect for others and their differences and for the power of love. The teachings show that we are all different but the power of love and commitment transcends all differences. A further dimension of the story is that it shows the importance of transmitting the teachings of Xeel's to future generations.

We are taken to the world long ago when fish and land animals could shift form and take on human-like qualities. The different species of fish emerged from the water one by one and removed their outer skins, which the storyteller calls "garments" and "masks," similar to the robes and masks people wear in the bighouse. Thinking of them in another way, they are like our outer selves, the face and body that we present to the world.

The Creator stressed the sacredness of our garments—our face and body—and the importance of respecting and guarding our garments. He reminded the old ladies of each clan to keep talking to the young ones about how sacred their garments were.

The Elders were passing on the importance of taking care of your outer layer, your face and body. They talked about the energy that surrounds us. It is slheyk'um'ews, the breath of the body. "Cover your mask so the energy on it won't be shared with others." What do you think they meant by this? It could mean to cover your body with clothing or regalia to keep it sacred and protected. Or it could mean to cover your body with white light so that your energy is contained within yourself and does not escape. The teachings show that we all have energy surrounding us, and that we can muster energy from other elements in the universe. Do you remember an occasion when you have chosen either to share, or not share, your energy?

Above all, we can understand the need to teach our children that they must look after their bodies because they are sacred. We can teach them that their bodies belong only to themselves and no one else. We need to find ways to teach our children to be strong in their minds so they will not give a part of themselves away. They will not have this awareness if they are not taught.

When finally the dog salmon arrived, Xeel's became excited and announced to the fish on the beach: "Your Elders are here, the k̓walúxw, the dog salmon. These are the great ones, your grandfathers and grandmothers." This story shows the importance of our Elders and the reverence we must hold for them. They pave our way. They carry the lessons from the past into the future. It is the job of the Elders, particularly the older women of the clan, to teach the young. In the past, the Elders would take the time to sit and discuss matters with the young people. Today, it seems as though we are losing this teaching time, and with it the lessons that the Elders pass on to future generations. What we teach our children ensures that they will never lose their way in this world. The lessons are many and varied, and can include the teachings of respect, compassion, understanding, acceptance, and love.

This story emphasizes the teaching that the fish, animal, and human worlds are all connected by universal energy. It tells about the differences among people and the huge mystery of love. In today's world, we can take these lessons and use them to become the collectors, historians, and teachers who are responsible for carrying the teachings forth to future generations.

Long ago, young people would learn at an early age that there are different types of fish and animals as well as different types of humans, and that they live in different places and have different cultures that must be respected. In today's world, recognizing that all cultures around the world are unique is just as important as recognizing that fish and animals have differences within each family.

In the story, we see many examples of respect. Just as Xeel's teaches the different fish to respect one another, so we can teach our children to respect other cultures and their ways. We also need to teach our children to respect sea life and animal life and also to respect their home—the earth. When we say we respect the salmon, we mean respecting everything about them, including keeping the rivers where they live clean, and honouring their spawning time. We need to understand how to help the sockeye survive, as well as the other species of fish and animals. We must all look after one another in this world: fish, animals, and humans, and all the living and non-living beings on this earth.

Xeel's spoke to the fish assembled on the beach, helping everyone see that all fish families are related. When the large spring salmon came, the Creator said to the sockeye, "Those are your big brothers and sisters." When the coho arrived, Xeel's heard that they were afraid of the other fish and were hesitating to remove their garments, so he whispered to them not to be afraid.

Fish families may look different and human families may look different from one another, but we must remember that we are all brothers and sisters. If we let the differences become more important than the similarities, the result is fear and mistrust.

As humans, we are different from the animals of the sea and land. Often, we show that we are afraid of them, which could make them afraid of us. Do you think this could be the cause of animals biting and killing humans? Biting is a way for animals to protect themselves. Do you think the situation among humans is similar? If a human is hit, he retaliates by protecting himself. Or a person who has been beaten may not retaliate against the aggressor, but may take it out on someone else without even knowing why. The teaching is that we are all related and must never hurt one another or be afraid of one another. We need to recognize that all of us around the world are related.

In the story, the Creator points out the importance of the fishes' slime, which he calls their "lifeline." One of the sacred teachings is the importance of your lifeline, your connection to your home and family and the place you are from. Your lifeline is like your DNA. If you fold your garment by itself, without the slime, you won't be able to put your garment back on. If you don't protect it and guard it, you won't be able to find your way home. So you must remember to keep the trail open, keep the lines of communication open.

The teachings of Xeel's on connections were very important. Xeel's said you must keep your connection to your home and family and home place. You must never forget where you come from. You must be aware that you have your lifeline, your slime, your connection. Without it, you could be lost, drifting in space, water, ocean, or even dreams. In your dream or vision state, your soul might drift away from your body, but if you are in tune with your lifeline, you can look back and you can see it there, connected to your belly button. If you want to go back to your body, your lifeline will take you back to where you left it. In today's world, you might feel adrift in a city, far away from your family and home village. You can think about your connection to your family; this is your lifeline. We must always honour our connection to family.

In the story, Xeel's advised all the salmon people that they would have many descendants who would be carrying their memories into the future. Honouring memory is another important teaching. The stories tell us that animals honour their past, and we as humans should honour ours as well. Do you believe that in today's world, we honour the past and carry our memories on to future generations?

Do we properly remember where our families come from and what their history is and how it may have affected them and ourselves? Also, we should be careful that the teachings don't become distorted as they are passed on generation after generation. We need to seek the teachings that must be carried forth.

This story shows an awareness and appreciation for Xeel's and his teachings. In the past, the old people coached the children to pray to Xeel's and acknowledge him. They taught them to call to him and then to listen. They taught the children to lift their arms to the heavens when they thanked him. They also coached the children not to think evil or be evil, as Xeel's knew their every thought. Also, they taught them to acknowledge the energy of the universe.

In the story, Xeel's watched while his children prepared to return to the ocean. When putting on their masks, they were careful to lift them to the four directions: north, south, east, and west. The four directions, the four energies of the universe, watch over all living and non-living things on Mother Earth. The energy of the universe encompasses all, and we are all connected by this universal energy.

On the fourth day, when it was time for all the fish to return to their homes, it became obvious to the Creator that the young sockeye had fallen in love with the young cod. The cod belonged to the deep ocean waters and would die in the fresh water of the river where the sockeye was going. So once again we see that they were from different worlds, and couldn't be together in either one.

However, the Creator offered the young sockeye an alternative. He asked if the sockeye would be willing to join him in the sky as a rainbow, to watch over his species. "I will stretch you and you will be called thuquI̓shúnum̓, the rainbow," Xeel's said.

The young sockeye told the Creator he would become thuquI̓shúnum̓ but he wanted his love to join him in the sky. The Creator had offered him an alternative. In our lives, there is always some alternative. If it is important enough, you will take the time to look at the choices you might have in life.

If the young sockeye became the rainbow, he would be able to help his family; and as it turned out, he could also have his love with him. The Creator told him how to bring his love Tl'useep to him, but warned the sockeye he would have to do this on his own. The Creator is there to walk with you and guide you. He can help, but you must do the actual work yourself.

Through the mingling of their tears and their bodies, the sockeye and the cod became one—thuquĺshúnuṁ. The mingling of their bodies can be seen as their own procreation as well as that of the many, many offspring who will carry the memories of past generations. The sockeye and the cod were thus able to help the sockeye's family in their journey, and their love was complete.

We must remember that in traditional teaching, these stories were spoken, not written. So the storyteller had the opportunity to focus on different aspects of the story as needed. He or she could highlight or expand different aspects as the student aged. Teaching about the different species of fish would lead to teaching about the different races in the world. Also, the importance of the sockeye spawning time could lead to discussions about love and procreation.

The ending of the story teaches that different species must not mingle, but it also portrays the importance of love's ability to overcome obstacles so you can obtain the true love you desire. The young sockeye was able to help his family reach the spawning grounds for eternity as well as join his love for eternity. The love of the sockeye and the cod was finally able to transcend the physical limitations they had faced, once they became the rainbow—thuquĺshúnuṁ.

The Marriage of the Seagull and the Crow

IN A VERY large village where everyone was related to one another, there was a family of qwuní, or seagulls. One of the qwuní grandfathers had married a cousin from his village. He had given this matter much thought and decided that marrying someone so closely related shouldn't happen in the future. As he walked along the rocks far away from the village he asked Xeel's, the Creator for support and help.

"Please give me a sign as to what we should do," the grandfather said. "Where will we find a wife for our precious grandson Qwunitun? I have been in communication with the family of a young woman in a village a few days away from here. These are very knowledgeable people. Could this girl be the one for our grandson?"

The people he spoke of were q̓ulé:q̓e', the crows. Grandfather Qwuní had been communicating with an Elder from the q̓ulé:q̓e' village. The qwuní and the q̓ulé:q̓e' knew how to send messages with their minds. Grandfather Qwuní knew that Grandfather Q̓ulé:q̓e' understood what he was feeling and what he wanted for his grandson.

"Grandfather Q̓ulé:q̓e' knows the problems we have had in the past because of intermarriages," he continued. "He has a granddaughter who is very knowledgeable for such a young crow. She is a medicine person, a healer, a midwife, and a communicator at all levels. She can communicate in the air as well as on land. She can communicate to our distant relatives who run on four legs and call them close, and they give themselves up to her.

"You, the great Creator of the universe, Xeel's, I am telling you all of this, I am telling you my concerns, because I know you understand. That is why I am asking you to please give me a sign, not for me, but for my grandson and the rest of my people and our people in the future."

He was so emotional, he cried as he walked back to the village. He flew at times, but he was so sad and felt so heavy he couldn't fly the whole way. When he did start to fly he could almost feel the energy of the wind peeling his sorrow away. He thought to himself, "What is happening to me? My face is twitching, my tongue is shivering, and my right wing is flapping on its own. That is the sign. I know I am going to be helped. I feel better."

He opened his mouth and hollered, "qwuníí, qwuníí," calling his people's name. The others came to meet him when he arrived at the village and they had a feeling that their Elder was happy. A few of the old ladies were gathered and they were taking apart the little crabs that would be their evening meal. It was their way to teach the young ones to bring them the little crabs, the little fish, and the bullheads.

"Aah huy', hay ch q̓a'," the old ladies said. "You young people will be so thanked by the grandfather when he eats. He might not remember to say 'hay ch q̓a',' but when he says 'ahhh' and nods his head, that is his way of sending you his love and appreciation. If we look after our special old people, it gives us strength, and it gives us energy, and therefore we receive knowledge. Watch closely when your Elders are speaking; watch how they move their heads and their arms. There are a lot of words unsaid. You will learn all of this through the teachings when we are all together."

Grandfather Qwuní was now seated outside. He never went directly inside; he always sat outside and closed his eyes for a while. He looked like he was falling asleep. When the children watched him he would laugh and gurgle "qaqaqaqa."

Grandmother Qwuní said, "He is laughing because he knows you are watching him and he knows what you are thinking, so enjoy it when you hear that."

The children waited until one of the grannies nodded at them and then the young ones brought out trays of food. The trays were made of inner cedar bark; the inner cedar bark was curved and tied at the ends, and that is what they put the food in. They liked to add a bit of liquid, salt water and fresh water, to make it easy to eat and swallow. It might be small chunks or big chunks of food, such as a crab or a spine from a fish, but it still went down easily.

When Grandfather Qwuní had finished eating, he began to give directions. He told the ladies to prepare food and put out the welcome mats. He told his grandson Qwunitun to get his cousins and go invite the Elders to a gathering. "Tell the younger ones to go and play so they won't be in the way; they don't need to know what the meeting is about."

The young people were moving fast. They knew something was going on, that there was going to be a meeting. They also knew that the Elders didn't want the children to hear what was being talked about at the meeting. In a way, the young people were hurt, but they respected the older ones and their wishes.

The adults told the children to go and gather shrimp around the point. An older person always went with them, especially if they were flying far up in the sky looking for shrimp. The young ones were excited when they were learning.

Also, the older ones knew how to communicate mentally with the creatures in the water. They knew the feeling and the energy of what they were looking for. The older ones were also teaching the young ones the differences in the energies they were feeling. The young ones were told to drink a lot of water and then spit it out in order to prepare the baskets in their throats where they carried their food. The children were very excited about learning and preparing.

In the village, the older women were also preparing for the meeting. They were bringing in food and laying it out on reed mats and in baskets, and some of the food was put in old clam shells, called čewiʔ. The old man was busy arranging his thoughts and planning the talks, planning the words so they came out right, so they were not repeated.

The guests arrived and were seated. Not saying a word, they sat and ate. They made noises as they ate: "Mmmmm, mmmmm." This was just their way. If they were too quiet they were not appreciating the food and not thankful for what they were eating. With the sounds of their enjoyment the host knew they were enjoying their food. The host didn't need to hear his guests saying "hay ch q̓aʼ, hay ch q̓aʼ." When the guests had finished eating, the spines from the sea urchin were passed around so they could pick their teeth, and at the same time enjoy the taste of the sea urchin.

The old man now stood up with his wife and co-wife (since he had more than one wife). When he spoke, he always included his family. His arms went out to his wives and his family, acknowledging their support. It was also important to let his guests know that his loved ones around him were aware of the importance of this gathering. He spoke about his concerns and he spoke of Xeel's, the Creator and the message Xeel's had given him.

"I had serious concerns," Grandfather Qwuní said, "and I asked for a sign. All of a sudden my face twitched, my tongue shivered, and my right wing moved on its own. That was a sign telling me not to do things on my own. That is why you are all here, my dear relatives. Please help us.

"You all know our relatives who live not too far away from here, the q̓ulé:q̓e'. I have communicated with one of their Elders and he informed me that one of their very knowledgeable girls is ready to marry. She is young but she is very strong. I have been praying for a mate who is not from this village for my grandson Qwunitun. He is not knowledge-able about mates yet, but if her family agrees, then at least we will have the girl here, and he will learn how to love her and get to know her. I have sent a message to the Elder there that we will come to ask for the young woman. We would like your blessings and we would like you to say whatever you want to say. We want to know if you agree with this or not. If you agree, we would like to have you come with us to the q̓ulé:q̓e' village."

Then one of the Elders from the village got up and said, "It is time to have another family join us. It is time to have a different family come into our village. We have been keeping to ourselves too much. We must have mixed energies. My family has also been talking, since we have young ones coming up, too. We know you have been praying about this. We all know what you want and we will support you. Whenever you say you want to go, we will go with you. We also have material goods to give as gifts to the q̓ulé:q̓e' Elders to support you and your family. I have also received a message from Xeel's, the Creator, the one who gives direction. I received a message that we should go forth into other nations. We will be stronger for it."

The old man who had been speaking was blind and they said he was deaf also, but when you were talking about something serious he knew what you were talking about. The villagers said, "Hay ch q̓a', aaahhhh, hay ch q̓a'."

One of the young fathers from another family asked Qwunitun's father, "Have you been talking to your son? We know he is a good hunter and he is a good communicator, but he doesn't communicate with us. Has he been trained to hold back his knowledge? Is that what it is?"

At that moment Qwunitun's father was shocked to realize that he had never communicated mentally with his son except while hunting. He realized that he had only taught his son about the different species of fish and how to communicate with Grandfather Water and Grandmother Earth. But he had not taught his son about the differences in the people of the air, had not taught him to communicate with others such as q̓ulé:q̓e', the crows.

The old blind man knew the thoughts of young Qwunitun's father. He felt very sad. The old blind man said, "We must train our young ones before they take a mate."

The grandfather of young Qwunitun said, "We all have deep concerns for our young. We must teach them. When we get the young crow here, we will sit and train our young ones in the appreciation of others."

The meeting had come to an end. Grandfather Qwuní thanked the people from the village and they departed. He thanked the old ladies and the other Elders who lived in the same house for their support and for the food that had been prepared. He told them to be prepared to leave at the fourth sunrise.

"I thank our ladies, since I know they will be gathering material goods for us to take to the other village. We will show our distant relatives, the crows, that we honour them, because they will be concerned about their young one. This has never happened before so we must realize how others feel about their own young. What I heard from our relatives who just left, and what I just realized myself, is we haven't been doing our job of teaching our young. One day they will take mates and they will have to know how to treat and appreciate the mates who will be providing the future generation. We have a lot of work to do."

Grandfather Qwuní prayed. He kept thanking the Creator and he said, "You have sent a message through a very old blind man to all of us. This is your way. The old man can't see or hear but he knows things. We must go forth into other nations and we will become stronger. We are not connecting with our young very well; we are not teaching them. We are not preparing them for life. We must prepare them to have a mate and then to have children. That was the message I've been looking for and we thank you. You have spoken to us through that old blind man."

They all bowed their heads and said hay ch q̓a' to Xeel's.

As they went to their nests, the words of Grandfather Qwuní made them think about the Elders of long ago who had worked so hard to train the future generations. They all sat on their little beds thinking about how they had forgotten to listen to the words of the Elders.

One of the old ladies thought, "That was what my great-grandmother always talked about. She talked about the importance of your inner thoughts and how you should save all the words from the old ones. When you need those words, all you have to do is bring the face of that very old person in front of you and you will remember. Even if they are gone a long time, they will get the message through to you. We were told to appreciate the message giver." She thanked the Elders from long ago as she fell asleep.

The young men worked hard over the next few days, gathering food and repairing their little houses. The young men said to Qwunitun, "Aren't you excited? We've been waiting for you to say something."

Young Qwunitun said, "I've been talking to you. What more should I say? What more do you want?"

His friends said, "Aren't you excited that in one sunrise you are going far away to see your new bride, your wife, the young girl, the black one with the red mouth?"

Young Qwunitun was absolutely shocked. He knew that the meeting was about something secret. He knew it was not a sacred meeting and he had a very bad feeling. He couldn't help himself. He quickly turned and pinned down the speaker, who was a cousin younger than himself, and he started picking at his eyes. "You tell me what you know or I will pick your eyes out."

One of the boys cried out, "Yuthust. Yuthust. Tell him. Tell him."

The boy on the ground looked at him and said, "Didn't you know? Hasn't your grandfather told you?"

"Told me what?"

"That you are going to that place where the q̇ulé:q̇e' live. You are going to get a black wife."

Qwunitun still had the young man pinned underneath him and he started to punch him. His cousin was bleeding and crying. The others jumped in and separated them and held Qwunitun back.

The boys said, "You can't do that to your relative. He is your brother. You will get into trouble with the Elders. We will have to make up a story that he fell asleep and fell out of a tree and injured himself, but you must promise to ask your father about this. Your father will tell you the truth. Hasn't your father told you that you are going to get a wife?"

"No," young Qwunitun said, "and I don't want a wife either!"

The boys explained to him, "You are the only one in your family. If you had a sister, then another family would take your sister away; but you are the only one. They expect grandchildren. They want grandchildren to take their place when they are gone. They always talk about s'uye?q (descendants). This is very important."

Young Qwunitun was very angry but he thought to himself, "My cousins will help me. I can run away. My cousins can hide me far away."

His older cousin said, "I know what you are thinking. You want us to help you run away. We will not do that. Our own grandfathers would be very angry with us. They might even know what we are talking about right now. I know this happens. We must go now."

When he arrived home, young Qwunitun became very quiet. He ate very little and went to his corner where he rested. His mother came and said to him, "You are very concerned about something, my son." He just nodded to her. She said, "I cannot help you with this, but remember that my heart is always with you and always will be, no matter where you are. I will send your father before he goes to rest and you can speak with him."

The father came quickly and said, "Our Elders have heard from the young ones about the talk you were having when you were gathering food. Also, they told me what happened to your cousin. It is a very important lesson that you must not beat your cousin, since he is your brother, your family. We must thank the Creator for teaching us this lesson. I am very happy that your cousins told you that they would not help you run away. We are leaving at first sunrise to go to the q̓ulé:q̓e' village to find a mate for you. We want a mate for you who is not qwuní. This is for your own future and the future of your children. Now, we will rest tonight."

Young Qwunitun said to his father, "I am not going to have any of those things that cry all the time, waiting for food."

The father looked at his son and said, "I am very sorry you feel that way. You must never say that or think that in front of your mother. It will make her very sad, because she cannot produce any more children. I still want her with me always as she is your mother and she is my life. It is very important to have a mate. I am sorry I have never spoken to you in this way. We should have been talking about this when you were small. We should have talked about the importance of the future. We will talk more about this once your new mate has arrived. But now you must rest, my son, because we are leaving in the morning and we are going to the village of our relatives, the crows. They might not accept us, since they will know how you feel. Do not damage our image. That is all I ask of you. We want to go there with good hearts." Then he left his son to rest.

But rest didn't come all night. Before sunrise, his mother came with a large clamshell full of nice little morsels of foods that he loved. It contained the beaks of the snails, the ends of the clams, and the little legs of the crab. All of this food he loved—but he couldn't swallow it. When his cousins came to see him they told him that three of them would be going with him on the trip, and they were told that they had to be with him at all times. He gave his food to them and they started to eat it happily and then one of the boys said, "I can't eat this food. Nucím'?—why?—nucím'?"

Another boy said, "When they bring you food especially prepared for you, it is only for you, it is like you have already eaten that food. But right now Qwunitun's whole body is angry and he can't eat it. In his body he is already married. I don't want a wife either, but they might get us wives from there, too."

"Give it to me," said another. "I will eat it. I am not scared. If they give me a wife, I will take her." They all laughed and they became a bit happier. Then they helped dress their cousin in a beautiful white cape lined with eagle down.

On the morning of departure everyone gathered at the canoes. They started packing all the situn (baskets), s̓qumuⱡ (paddles), and thuⱡshutun (mats) into the canoe. Young Qwunitun looked at everything gathered and he thought, "No one is that expensive—situn, thuⱡshutun, s̓qumuⱡ. No one is worth that much!"

Hardly anyone spoke. The fathers were trying to talk, trying to make things easier and happier. The boys didn't want to think, because they knew the grandfather would know what they were thinking. They kept teasing young Qwunitun. When they ate they left the red huckleberries in their mouth and they made sounds like crows. Their mouths were all red and they kept making sounds. They were teasing him, "This is how your wife is going to look."

When they went to bed and rested among the trees, they again made the sounds of the crow. Young Qwunitun was very angry and he went to another tree to be by himself. The next day was the same. Finally, on the last day of the trip, Grandfather stopped earlier than usual and they sat around eating, telling stories and jokes, and of course the young cousins teased young Qwunitun.

Grandfather told everyone to be quiet. He talked to young Qwunitun as he looked directly at him. "Do you know why your grandmother put that blanket and mat there for you? Because today and this night you must be thinking about yourself and your future. Go to a tree by yourself and think about yourself and your life. You are not a child anymore. You are a young qwuní man and it is now time for you to have a mate and a family.

"You must be alone most of the night. Do not talk to your cousins. We want you to appreciate and be thankful to your family and family members that are here to support you. You must pray to the Creator that you will be honoured and you will be given the young girl.

"It would be an embarrassment to our whole family if they refuse us. This canoe full of gifts will be pulled up to their beach, canoe and all, for the q̓ulé:q̓e'. They will be given the gifts to keep, and they can give them away or do whatever they want to do with them, even if we are refused. And, if they refuse you, then you will have to take one of your older cousins as a wife."

Everyone was very quiet. Qwunitun didn't ask why. He didn't say that he didn't want to go through with this. He just stayed quiet. It was coming to the point now that he felt whatever he did or said didn't matter since they were going to tell him what to do anyway. "They will just say, 'This is the way,' even if I think it is not *my* way," he thought. He had never prayed to Xeel's, the Creator except when he wanted to catch the fattest deer and the biggest salmon. That was the only time he prayed and that was all he wanted in life. So he left and went away from the camp and slept. He was happy that he was not with his cousins.

The next morning they were all up before the sun, feeding, praying, and singing, and then they left. As they set out, they looked back, saying thank you to the place they had camped, and apologizing for any disturbance they might have caused. They prayed that their leavings would be useful where they lay.

As he prayed, Qwunitun thought to himself, "Am I learning? Why are they saying that? Why am I saying that? I wasn't happy in that place. I am angry. Yet we are thanking that place for allowing us to stay there overnight."

The sun was up when they rounded the point. There, two q̓ulé:q̓e' canoes waited for them. The q̓ulé:q̓e' told the qwuní to go ashore. "There is nourishment for you there," the q̓ulé:q̓e' said. "Our women are preparing food for you."

The qwuní went ashore and ate, sang songs, and prayed. Grandfather told them to go into the woods but to be careful where they placed their leavings, to leave them in a good place so the woods would not be harmed.

"You will be sitting for a long time," Grandfather said, "and you won't be able to leave the circle. So take care of what you need to."

The qwuní all did what they were told and then got into their canoe. The canoes from the q̓ulé:q̓e' village led them without saying a word.

The q̓ulé:q̓e' were all black. Qwunitun couldn't help looking at them, especially the women. "How ugly their bottoms are," he thought. "Like mink, all puffy and red. Are they sick? What's wrong with them? Their bottoms are red and their mouths are always open. All you can see are their eyes rolling but nothing beyond, just blackness." He could smell them. His grandfather moved his head slowly and looked directly at Qwunitun. He knew that his grandfather was reading his mind. He just looked down and tried to stop thinking.

How could he not think? He tried and tried. He was getting the message from his grandfather, "Look at the bubbles that the paddles make. The bubbles have air in them, count the bubbles." He counted from the smallest to the largest and they seemed to be making noise. He was amazed that these things were alive, as if they were talking, teasing. Or was he going crazy? He had heard of qwuní going crazy before.

They were coming close to the shore now. Some old people were sitting on the logs and some were walking back and forth on the logs. They seemed to be the masters. There was one q̓ulé:q̓e' who walked back and forth on the beach. He was totally black. He motioned the qwuní to shore and they all got off their canoe. They gathered on the beach and made a fire and leaned against the logs and waited. They were left alone.

Evening came and they were still there alone. Darkness came and then they could see dark eyes in the bushes. They knew there were guards surrounding them. Every time the young men wanted to relieve themselves the old ladies would direct them, "Go behind me, don't go too far away." Then the old ladies would gather the leavings and wrap them up. Nothing was left on the beach.

They ate very little. They slept very little. When the sun came up, they drummed on the logs and sang a song expressing thanks for the coming day, thanking the maker of this earth, the Father, the giver of light and the giver of life.

Somehow Qwunitun remembered those songs. He remembered them from a time when he had gone to another village with his uncle when he was just a young child. He recalled that on that day, he had a new auntie. She had said to him, "Don't call me cousin anymore, call me nikw (auntie), call me nikw." He remembered that day. "Oh," he thought, "that is when Uncle went and got our cousin as a wife. That is what is happening right here, right now!"

They finished eating the food that was given to them by the q̓ulé:q̓e'. Then an old crow lady came to them. She was hiding food under her cape. She didn't say anything but just dropped a situn full of food by their grandmother. They nodded at each other and she left. Then an older man came and motioned them to follow. He spoke their own words; he could understand them and he called them into the bighouse.

When they got inside they were told to sit by the door and there was drumming and singing. The Elders sat in the front and the young ones in the back.

A few of the ladies came forward with trays of food and they put them in front of the Elders. They ate and appreciated the food and when they finished, the Elders told them to thank their hosts for what they had received. They got the drums out and drummed a hay ch q̓a' song. Some of the mothers got up and danced, their beautiful arms going out to their sides, their heads going up and down. When they sat down they covered up again. They were covered in dark material, as they didn't want to look too white; they wanted to show respect to the black people. They stayed there until the sun was going down.

Some of the young qwuní were starting to get restless. The grandmother said, "Do it in the situn and I will clean it up." Each one took a turn without fuss, going behind the grandmothers who fixed the blankets, hiding the young ones. This was done out of respect for the bighouse since only a few of the old ladies were allowed to go outside. The grandmothers went down to the beach, washed the baskets in the water, and thanked the water for taking the leavings away.

The sun was almost down when people started to come in, all following one another in a line. Two big fires were built in the middle of the floor. Mats were put on the dirt floor and then blankets were put on top of the mats. The blankets were beautiful, made of soft inner cedar bark. The reed mats were woven with feathers, black, grey, white.

Qwunitun thought to himself, "Where did they get all of this?" His mind was going so fast and once in a while his grandfather would look back at him and his mind would go to rest again.

The speaker from the q̓ulé:q̓e' family got up and said, "Welcome. I would like to welcome the families who are sitting by the door. Come and sit here between these fires, come and sit with us." They brought clamshells full of juice to the qwuní who drank it, licking their beaks, and making noises to show their appreciation.

The old man from the q̓ulé:q̓e' family said, "We would like to hear from your Elder. Why have we been honoured with your journey to come here? As you know from the past, your people have always shunned us. We want to know why you are here now."

Grandfather Qwuni stood. He wasn't prancing back and forth, he was calm, showing no arrogance. He said, "We have journeyed far. Before we left our village we had a gathering and I expressed my concern to my people about our intermarriages. We want that to end. We asked Xeel's, the Creator to help us. We received messages and signs that told us it is time for a change. We heard messages that you have one young woman that is ready for a mate, that she is knowledgeable, from highly esteemed and honoured people. We ask you and we beg you for her as a mate for our grandson. We would be so happy and honoured if you would consider giving her to us.

"We have here a very knowledgeable grandson. He is knowledgeable in the ways of hunting so she would never be hungry, knowledgeable in the ways of gathering to make things, and in harvesting and preparing food for the winter when hard times come. He is learning to communicate with people far away. He is learning the words of the water and the energy of the universe that is given to all things. It is time for him to have a mate and we would be honoured if you would consider giving her to us. That is why we have come to see you. We will now leave you so you can talk alone. Hay ch q̓a'."

The qwuní family left the bighouse and built a fire on the beach and they all slept in a little circle. Before the sun came up, the qwuní fathers went and spoke to the q̓ulé:q̓e' fathers in the village. The qwuní found the biggest men from the village and asked them to help. They put cloaks on the men and paid them very well. These men were chosen to carry the canoe filled with the material goods up the beach to the village. They laid mats alongside the canoe and then the qwuní sang the hay ch q̓a' song.

"Hay ch q̓a' that you allow us to bring these gifts to you. If you do not give us what we ask for, these gifts will still be yours and you can give them to your relatives. These gifts are yours. Hay ch q̓a'. Hay ch q̓a'."

The q̓ulé:q̓e' family had been awake for a long time preparing food. The door to the bighouse opened and it looked different in the house. It looked happier, felt happier. The q̓ulé:q̓e' family waved them in. There was a raised platform covered with mats for them to sit on. Then the men packed the canoe in and brought it to the middle of the floor and put it down. When the men left they bowed and walked backwards to the door.

When the qwuní family were seated, they were fed. Grandfather Q̓ulé:q̓e' said, "We are honoured that you have come this far. We were up all night and we have relatives here now advising us. We have talked and we believe this is a good proposal. We are happy to accept your proposal to take our young lady called Qu'le. We want you, young man, to come and sit on these blankets."

Qwunitun thought, "Am I just going to walk up there? What am I supposed to do?"

Then his grandfather motioned for him to stay seated. Grandfather Qwuní went to the door and called the four big q̓ulé:q̓e' men who had helped bring the canoe in, and the women clothed them in big beautiful capes. The women next cloaked Qwunitun and put red ochre on his cheeks, beak, and wings, which marked him as a member of the highly esteemed family.

The grandfather said to the four q̓ulé:q̓e' men, "I want you to bring my grandson to the platform." The four men took Qwunitun by the arms and lifted him to the platform and sat him there.

There was another seat there and he looked and thought, "Oh, they are going to bring her in. The other seat is for her."

He wanted to get sick but he remembered his teaching: Remove yourself, you are not yourself. He tried this and then he could feel himself becoming calmer and he felt as though he was not himself. He was happier. He asked himself, "What happened?

I am not me anymore." He sat there looking around and then stared at the fire.

Qwunitun looked calmer and his cousins thought, "He is so calm. He looks happier. What happened?"

The door at the back of the bighouse opened and there was drumming and singing, like it was far away. Then it grew louder and a beautifully cloaked young woman, Qu'le, came in held by older women, but she was struggling to get away. It was the way of a long time ago but Qwunitun didn't know this. Qu'le kept struggling and when they reached the platform they raised her up and then they seated her next to him. She wouldn't look at him; she looked away in the other direction.

He thought to himself, "She is not even here. She is just a thing sitting beside me." He liked it that way.

The dancing went on and the speeches went on. He heard his grandfather talking about his appreciation and the future, and how they could help one another and support one another. No more famine on either side of the family since they would all look after one another. They would use their minds to communicate with one another when they needed help. They would help the crow family and the crow family would help the seagull family. The dancing went on and the eating went on and the speeches went on. Then somebody came and put a cloak over both of them. He didn't care. He thought, "That is the way they do it. Let them do it. I am not here."

At the end of the long night of celebration, Qwunitun's family went back to the beach. Early the next morning the canoe filled with gifts was outside on a raised platform. It would stay there for everyone to see and admire, so everyone could say thank you to the mighty qwuní family who had come and honoured them.

Now other canoes were being loaded with gifts, such as dried food, clams, fish, and berries. One canoe had baskets filled with Qu'le's belongings, along with clothes for her husband. There were baskets of herbs and medicines, since she was a medicine person. The q̓ulé:q̓e' family covered her head; the qwuní family didn't do this, but the q̓ulé:q̓e' did. In this way she wouldn't be in sorrow and she wouldn't grieve as she left her village—this was their way.

They wanted Qwunitun to sit with her and he did for a short time. Then he said, "I want to paddle." He was already finding ways to be away from her. His sisters and cousins would stay with her and sleep with her in the woods. The old ladies were quite happy that he didn't want to have anything to do with her right away. They had to watch her for two moons. When she got her moon, they would know she was not already pregnant.

They had only been at home a few nights when Qwunitun started to pack. Someone told his grandfather and he sent for his grandson right away. The old man called his older relatives to sit there while he spoke to the young man. The grandfather already knew deep in his heart that something was terribly wrong. He talked to Qwunitun about being a grown man, and told him that it was time for him to have his own family now.

"I am never going to have a family," Qwunitun said. "I am going away, far away, and I'm never going to come back. You people wanted her. You, father, you wanted her. You, grandfather, you wanted her. Now you can have her. I don't want her. I never wanted to be close to anybody so black. I imagine that she stinks. I've seen her several times sitting with her legs apart and I see that red ass of hers. I went to watch her sleep and she doesn't sleep like my female cousins. My cousins sleep so delicately, so calmly and so beautifully. This one, when you look at her, you want to get sick. Why would I want to be close to something like that?"

The grandfather said to him, "We haven't talked to you about being intimate with any female. We haven't talked to you about producing the next generation."

Right off Qwunitun said, "You make the next generation. I don't even know how *I* came to be."

The grandmothers huddled together and hugged one another, weeping. They looked at one another and said, "What have we done?" The old man could hear their sorrow. He also blamed himself. He hadn't taught his grandson how to be with his new mate. Why did he think this was going to be so different when his grandson hadn't been taught anything?

The young fellow gathered his belongings and said, "I am going!"

Grandmother Q̓ulé:q̓e' had arrived to help her granddaughter get settled, and to continue with her teachings of the spiritual and sacred ways of life. Grandmother Q̓ulé:q̓e' and Grandmother Qwuní looked at one another and motioned each other to the door. They quickly went to get Qu'le.

How had they known this was going to happen? They just knew, and they already had a parcel packed.

Grandmother Q̓ulé:q̓e' had the herbs and medicines packed and all the things that would make life easier. Qwunitun's grandmother had a bag filled with string to be used to tie clothing, and sharp little bones to use as needles to puncture material to make footgear and shelter. They didn't hug her or touch her. There was a reason for this: they didn't want their heaviness going with her. They motioned her outside and she followed. Qu'le was now packing the essentials and the useful articles that her grandmothers had packed for her.

Qwunitun knew when he reached the top of the hill that someone was following him. He threw rocks at Qu'le so she stayed far behind. Now she was communicating with Grandfather Qwuní. Qwunitun could barely communicate with his own grandfather through air, but this young girl was able to receive his direction easily.

Grandfather Qwuní said, "You see that point in the mountain? You might think he went that way, but he is trying to fool you. He is really going the other way, through the swamp. You know how to get across the swamp without getting wet."

She knew what to do and she didn't even have to answer him, since he knew what she was thinking.

He knew that she had been praying to Xeel's, the Creator when she was by herself. She knew her ancestors were close to her, even though they had been gone a long time. It became their job now to follow her and help her.

Qu'le knew that once she and Qwunitun went over the mountain it would get very cold. She gathered wool that was stuck to the branches, and she gathered feathers from nests, one by one. She was very selective, and put them all in her bag. She prayed to the air, the sun, and the moon. She called them the ancestors. She prayed that Qwunitun would change his mind and think kindly towards her.

But she knew that even now if he jumped into the water or off a high cliff or if he was in a fire, she would save him. She knew that once she was married to him she would stay with him for life. That was the lesson, the teachings she had heard. The swamp didn't bother her; the swamp seemed to be telling her that it would help her. She knew then that anywhere she went she would be helped. She had the feeling that the trees protected her when she took shelter. They said to her, "Take our limbs and make shelter." Even if Qwunitun didn't help her she would be helped by everything surrounding her. She knew this from that feeling deep inside herself.

Qwunitun didn't stop, but kept on going and they reached colder and colder mountains. Mountain after mountain, she couldn't count anymore. She bathed in the streams and asked for forgiveness, as she knew they were the first to journey there.

Then she saw creatures that looked like her but they were bigger than her and they were different. Spa:l̓ (raven) welcomed her into their territory.

"What are you to me?" she asked.

"We are the grandfathers."

They were very big and she knew not to become too friendly with them.

She said, "I am following him."

The ravens said, "We will help you but we can't help him."

Qwunitun had spoken to them also and he apologized for passing amongst them and disrupting their territory. He apologized for having to kill little things like rats and squirrels even though he didn't leave anything behind. He kept the skins, as he knew that one day he would need them to wrap his feet even though he didn't know how to make proper foot coverings. He remembered his grandmother making him something to cover his feet. He thought, "I have the skin. I will just wrap my feet then I will throw the skins away when I am finished with them. There are a lot of rats around."

Somehow he didn't like the name of these animals. Rats are called hewt. He never questioned his grandfather when he was being taught about the spiritual ways of the animals. In his mind he was the only one that knew anything about communicating; he was the only one that was important.

"It will come. I am special because I was taught by my grandfather."

That is why the trees looked away from him. They felt sorry that he would let the person who was following him do everything for herself. She even made a shelter for herself when it was very wet and cold.

One day Qu'le saw Qwunitun making a shelter and she knew they were going to stay in that spot for a while. She proceeded to make her own shelter, which was very comfortable and warm. She made a nice big fire and she knew he would come, because he needed to warm up. She could see that he was very cold. Snow was coming, she could feel it. In the middle of the night, she heard someone putting wood on the fire. She looked out and said, "It is very warm in here if you want to come in."

She could see that he was shivering, so she offered him a cover and he took it. She comforted him and he allowed her to. In the dark one night when he was close to her, she found his hands moving all over her and she allowed that, because she was so lonely for companionship. When he left in the morning, he said, "Thank you for allowing me to comfort myself."

He never said, "to comfort you." It was always, "to comfort myself." She would leave food outside and he would take it and go away. When he made a kill he would take the best parts for himself and think, "This part is for her, the big mouth." When she called him "Qwunitun" he didn't like that. He said, "Don't call me by my name. I don't even know you."

When he came to her at night, she knew what he was doing, probing and feeling. She knew that he wanted to get closer to her but he didn't know how. She became very frustrated. He came in and out night after night. When he came close to her at night, especially early in the morning, his hands would roam all over her. She knew that he wanted to get very close to her and she guided him, yet when he penetrated her he said, "What are you doing to me?" Then he would run outside, talking to himself, that he never wanted to get close to that black thing with the big mouth. She knew that he didn't know how to get close to her, to touch the female parts. He didn't know where to put his male part.

After that he looked at her in a funny way when he visited. He was always looking at her bottom and she knew what he was thinking. He was looking and seeing.

They didn't move from that area for the longest time. It was deep winter now. He would bring her food and she would cook it and there were no words between them. He said to her one time, "When I was young and we went swimming with my cousins, the female bottoms were so beautiful."

She didn't answer him. Then one day she said to him, "We are different but to have close contact and penetration, it would be as if we are the same. We are not that different."

He didn't say anything but he knew he had penetrated her many times. One day she said, "I will not be moving away from here for a while."

Qwunitun said, "Are you sick? Are you going to die?" She was wearing covers a lot and she was cold.

He said, "Go get your own wood if you are cold." She didn't want him to get close to her now and he was mad, he was angry. He kept saying, "You better pack up and go home. Go to your own family, you know where they live. If they still want you. You are acting so weird it seems as if you are from another world."

All she said to him was, "Oh my dear, we live in the same world, and we have to remember that."

He didn't like it when she spoke because she seemed to know what she was talking about. "The person that knows everything! She thinks she is better than me."

One day he came to the shack, which was quite comfortable now, and something was moving around and crying in the hut. He went and looked and saw this thing. He could see that it was just about all black with a bit of white on it.

"Where did you get this thing? Get it out of here! It's dirty. Go and put it back where you found it. Go throw it away. I don't want to look at it!"

"That is our first one," she said.

Qwunitun didn't know what she was talking about. "First one of what? Get rid of it."

She said to him, "It is yours also."

As he was walking out the door he said, "I don't want it. Go throw it away wherever you found it."

The little fellow was so understanding. Even though he was only a few days old he was already talking and helping his mother.

When the nights were cold, Qwunitun would come into the little hut to get close to her. She asked him, "Do you know what you are doing when you come and lay down beside me? Do you know what that means?"

"I come to relieve myself just like when I go to the bushes to relieve myself. You are just there. Isn't that what you are for?"

She knew she was going to have another little one. The first one just wanted to stay out of his father's way. When his father came in, the little one went out. He was a kind and brave little one, always helping his mother.

One day Qwunitun came in and had something to eat, and he started to praise her for the first time. "What am I eating? This is very good."

Qu'le said, "That is what he made for you."

He looked and said, "That thing?" He grabbed some of the food and left without saying another word.

The mother never had to say she was sorry to her young son. She looked at her son and nodded and the young boy just nodded at her. He understood.

When the next one was born, the body was mainly white. When Qwunitun saw the little one he said, "Now where did you get this one? I am going to leave. Every time I come in, you have another one. I am getting tired of hunting to feed those mouths."

The oldest one said, "I will be old enough to hunt for our food soon."

"I wasn't talking to you," the father said. "Don't ever talk to me."

The little boy said, "My mother has been teaching me how to make spears and a bow and arrow."

Qwunitun said, "All you are going to do is shoot one another with it. You don't know how to do anything. You are always waiting for me to bring food home."

Qu'le shook her head and said, "Aa si'ém̓ (my dear one)."

Then Qwunitun went away for a long time. When he came home, there were two more small ones added to the family.

"You had two! Now you have another two? Who is giving you these? Why?"

"It is just the way it is. If I was somewhere else by myself I wouldn't get them."

"Why are you getting them?"

"You are giving them to me when you lay down with me."

"I give you nothing. I never wanted to give you anything."

Their first boy began to hunt while the father was away and he would bring home his catch. Even a mouse made a nice barbeque. He knew a family of mice and rats and they gave themselves to him. The rats said, "We know, we know. Your mother is from far away and your father doesn't want you. We will look after you. We will give ourselves to you when you need us."

The little boy could barely drag the rats home. Sometimes he would make two trips because he didn't want to waste even a bit of the skin. He even collected the blood so no blood would be left on Mother Earth. His mother taught him, "Don't damage Mother Earth with the blood from your kill. Just pray your kill doesn't suffer and we will not become ill when we eat it and also Mother Earth will not become ill."

Even the eyes made a big meal for them. Qu'le would put hot rocks in the basket of water and the water would boil the eyes and she would give the juice to the new ones. The new ones were even helping by collecting wood for their evening meal. The eldest boy was getting big; he was even taller than his mother now.

He said to his mother, "Is it because he is different from you, is that why we are different?"

She said, "Even if you are different, my love for you will never change. If your grandparents saw you they would love you just as I do."

"Thank you, Mother. When I look at me I am just about like you. My brother is mostly white and bigger than me. The twins are small and have different coloured eyes. Thank you for loving us the way we are."

Sometimes the young ones played a game of how they would one day go to that faraway place where their great-grandparents lived. "Our great-grandparents will call us qwuní and q̓ulé:q̓e' and they will love us."

Then they heard a voice speaking to them, "Yes. Nemʔts tseʔ awʔ souʔqʔthamu' (we are going to look for you)." They looked at one another in surprise, even the smallest ones, the twins. Mother always called them "the two"; their eyes were so big and had many different colours.

The boys wanted to look outside to see if their great-grandparents were there. "Where are they?" The mother told them that their great-grandparents were talking to them in their minds and they would find them one day.

In the meantime, Qwunitun was hunting way up in the hills and he was talking to himself. He didn't care if the trees or sacred rocks heard him. "I have so many mouths to feed now. How many are there? There are so many I can't even count them anymore. Every time I look at her, the biggest mouth of all, she is bringing home another one. Now there are two new ones and they have different coloured eyes. Where is she picking these things up? I don't know. She says I must feed them. I must clothe them. Was I brought into this world for that reason? I must have done something very wrong when I was young to be punished. I have no Creator, no Xeel's. I don't believe in him but she does—the biggest mouth of all. She has a bigger mouth than the two little ones put together."

He looked up from his grumbling and there was a man standing on the trail at a crossroad. "It isn't one of us," he thought. "It is one of those things that appears to be walking on legs; it doesn't fly, it is glued to the ground."

The man approached him and said, "Aa si'ém̓. Are you hunting?"

"If I knew you, I would answer you but I have never seen you before so I am not going to tell you what I am doing."

"Aa si'ém̓."

"Why are you calling me that?"

"That means 'I recognize you, dear one.'"

"I haven't seen you anywhere before and I have travelled a long way."

Qwunitun left the man and started to walk away and as he was walking away he could hear the man saying, "If you follow that trail and go up the hill there are some deer there."

Qwunitun didn't look back. He didn't answer. He just kept on walking. "He is one of the nosy ones. If I see him again I'll tell him to go away." He continued to talk to himself about the little ones in his hut. Now he was calling the hut that Qu'le had made "his hut." They were always there waiting in "his hut" with the biggest mouth of all, their mother.

When he looked up from his grumbling there was a herd of deer walking, looking at him. He fixed his bow and arrow. One of the deer didn't move; it kept eating something. What was it eating? What could it be eating? What was he thinking about? There wasn't any grass on this trail but this deer was eating something. The deer had beautiful strong antlers he could use for a knife for the young ones. "Why am I thinking about them? Those boys are always making something for themselves, making things— and they'll never be hunters, not with that mother. She keeps them under her wing all the time and she never leaves them alone with me. But I am the one that doesn't want to be alone with them! Why am I thinking about them?"

The other deer were walking away, but still the one deer stood there. Qwunitun pretended to be part of the foliage, not making a sound, doing what his grandfather taught him. "Think that your feet are covered with fluff from the cottonwood or dande- lion." He used to go up into the mountain to gather dandelion fluff, and the flowers were white and beau- tiful and the roots were good to eat. His grandmother always gathered the roots and she would feed them to him when his back or stomach was sore.

While he was thinking, the deer came very close to him. He should be praising this animal that stood in front of him. "Why am I thinking that?" He lifted his bow and arrow and without really thinking, the arrow was already gone. It was aimed right for the heart of this animal that stood and offered himself. The animal lay down. He ran and poked at the animal. It was dead. It usually takes two or three arrows to bring down such a huge animal.

"I am so good," he said to himself. "I am so great." He lifted his big wings to the sky and jumped, hopped, and flopped around. "Look at me, the stars who are my friends. Look at me, qwunus, the whale, who lives in the ocean. You are the biggest thing in the water but you cannot kill an animal, but I did, with one arrow." He hopped around dancing, singing his family name. "Qwuní, qwuní, qwuní." He moved the animal to a little hill so it would be easy to drain its innards. He took out his cherished knife made of bone.

Qwunitun spoke to the deer. "This knife is the bone of your grandfather. I loved your old grandfather. I still thank him because he was my first kill."

He was now humble again. He touched the animal with kindness. As he put the knife in and started to cut, it was so easy. He amazed himself. He took out the innards and stretched the intestine, which he would use to make rope. He kept saying, "Aa si'ém̓ smuyuth (deer)." And then he would say, "I am the best in the world!" He cut to the inside of the deer which is fatty. The fat that surrounds the kidney is called 'anuẇ. Qwunitun started to gather the 'anuẇ and put the chunks into little pouches in his belt.

"This is for the little one that always has snot hanging from his nose. This is for another one, the one that pees himself all the time. And this is for the one that cries all the time; even though he is big, he is sloppy when he walks. And then, this is for the one that is like her, the biggest mouth of all. When I talk to him, he goes 'hhhmm' just like his mother."

Qwunitun continued to put little pieces of suet into the pouches, but he didn't even know his children's names. Then he began to think about all the good things he was able to do for himself. He saved some of the liver for himself and some of the bladder too. He would use this to catch fish. He would put this ugly stuff at the end of the line and the fish would go to sleep after they ate it. He collected devil's club spines to put on the end of his fishhooks. When he wanted to catch caterpillars and butterflies, he strung a line and they landed on it and got hooked.

Then he asked for their help. "Help me to journey far away in my mind, so I can see what is happening at the end of the world." He had learned how to do that from his grandfather. He was taught well that way.

He would close his eyes halfway and see far away. He would call butterfly and moth, who were his friends. He also praised the owl because it can see at night and so can he. He hopped around and thought about all the good things he had done to help himself.

The deer was now cleaned and he gathered ferns to clean the blood. He was still talking about what he was going to be doing for himself while he gathered the ferns to sop up the blood. Then he fastened the deer's right legs together. First he cut a hole in the end of the back leg; then he threaded the hoof of the front leg through, making a kind of ring. He dragged the deer and put it on a log so it would be easy to get underneath. He lifted the deer onto his back and put his arms through the tied-up legs and that was how he carried it. His little legs were twisting this way and that and he could barely walk. He staggered along and he came to the crossroads again and there was the man he had seen before. The man tried to stop Qwunitun but he wouldn't stop.

"Can I help you, my son?"

"I am not your son!"

"Where is your bow and arrow?"

This man was irritating him but Qwunitun couldn't walk any more. He backed up against a log but he didn't take the deer off his back. The deer was very heavy but he was trained to take it home in one piece. If you do, the deer will like you because you are honouring it. If you cut it up, you are scattering its life, and deer will never give themselves to you again.

He continued to rest and he could see that the man was walking towards him. He thought, "He is so big. If it wasn't me, I would be so scared, but it is me, and I'm scared of no one because I am Qwunitun."

Xeel's walked up to Qwunitun and said, "Ah, my son, I am glad you are resting. Do you have any of that liver? Can I have just a little chunk of your liver? I don't eat very much."

"Look at your hands. You have long hands and legs. And what do you do? You just walk around bothering people."

"Can I help you with your pack?"

"You go away! You know how to get things from people but you aren't getting anything from me!"

But then Qwunitun started to dig in his pouch and he cut a piece of the liver off. He would normally get straw and grass and a leaf and hand it to an old person that way, but right now he was angry. He threw the liver down on the ground and the old man went and picked it up. He had a little cloth, deer hide, an ugly little thing, and he wiped the liver off.

"Thank you, my son," he said as he kissed the liver. This made Qwunitun sick. Xeel's wrapped up the liver and put it in the bag he was carrying.

The man walked with a long stick that looked dirty and old. "It must be from the arbutus tree, qa:nlhp, because it looks so heavy," Qwunitun thought. Deep in his heart he wished he were big so he could carry this heavy stick, and then he could use it to hit somebody on the legs, somebody tall and big. He remembered he was angry with this man. "I must go."

"Oh, you have saved the suet for your beautiful children and your wife."

"How do you know them?" Qwunitun glared at Xeel's. His eyes were like big balls of fire. "Where did you see her?"

"I know everyone."

"How do you know I have children?"

"I know everything, my son."

"I still don't know how you know that woman and those children of hers."

"They are beautiful and they love you. I am only here to help. I just want to pray on your pack so it becomes lighter."

Qwunitun started running because he wanted to get away from this intrusive man who kept showing up. He wouldn't look back. He didn't want to see him again. How did the man know this woman? Maybe he found those ugly things for her. He ran and ran until he got close to home. He knew there would be a fire. They would all be around the fire waiting for the suet and she would be waiting, the biggest mouth of all.

He always sat on the same log outside the hut when he got home. He could see that the fire was burning. Yes, those boys must have been collecting wood. That's the only thing they did was collect wood for her. He dropped his smuyuth on one of the logs. He could feel the antler on his wing as he moved away from the burden he was carrying. He went into the little lelum̓ (house) and there they were.

"I knew it! I knew it! I just knew where you would be sitting. Waiting with your mouths open. Take the snot off your face. It makes me sick to look at you. This is what you've been waiting for." He started to throw the pieces of food he had saved at the children.

"Aaahhhhh," cried the smallest boy.

He threw a pouch at another one and knocked him over on his back. "Now you are showing me your ugly feet. Don't show them to the universe."

The pouch fell over. Qu'le picked it up and said, "Don't you ever get tired of doing this to your children?"

He said, "They are not mine. They don't even look like me."

Qu'le looked in the pouch and saw there were only jagged rocks inside. She looked inside the other pouches and they too contained only rocks. She ran towards her children and they started coming to her. They said, "Mother, let's get out of here!"

Qwunitun said, "Stop that crying. You will all be like the one with snot hanging from his nose. Get out there and get the deer and cook me something. Here is the liver—cook it."

Qu'le went to get her knives and the trays she had made from the bark of cedar. Even at this moment she remembered to thank everything that she used. She looked for the deer and the lump outside looked like a deer, but it wasn't. It seemed to be rotten old wood. She went into the lelum̓ and asked Qwunitun, "Where is the deer?"

"What do you mean, where is the deer? It's outside. Where is my food?"

"Aa si'ém̓. There is no deer out there."

"I put it on the log outside."

"There is only a stump out there. It looks like a deer but it isn't."

"I knew it. It's that ugly old man that keeps bothering me! I should have killed him."

"You must mean our grandfather, Xeel's."

"Xeel's, my spoo (shit). He did it and you know him. He gave you those ugly things."

"Yes, we all come from him."

"I am going to find him and kill him."

Qwunitun was furious and he began to look for his weapons. He was gathering his weapons in a frenzy. His bow and arrow and spear were dragging on the ground as he ran around.

Suṅtl?e', the eldest boy, said, "Mother, we have been hiding food on the other side of the point. We have clothing, we have bedding. We want to take you away from here. You told us to go towards the sun, our grandfather, and he would help us to find our real grandparents. We were just waiting for another winter to pass and then we were planning to take you away. We have been learning to hunt and we have been drying fish and we have everything at our hiding place."

Qu'le wanted to sit and cry but Suṅtl?e' said, "There is no time. We must leave."

The other boys said, "We must listen to Suṅtl?e'. He is very good, he teaches us. We don't tell Father because he would get mad at us."

Qu'le started to quietly gather just a few of her belongings, her favourite knives, her sewing basket, and some of the roots she had saved, and then they started to run. When they got to the hiding place, she was amazed to see everything her children had collected: bows and arrows, knives, skins prepared beautifully to use as cover while they travelled. They had even made foot covers in case they had to spend time in the snowy mountains. They had thought of everything.

They all gathered their packs and started to run. Qu'le wanted to stop and pray but she thought she had better do that while she was running. Her sons didn't run too fast because they didn't want their precious mother to get tired.

In the meantime, Qwunitun had gone close to the crossroad where he had first met Xeel's. And there he was again, standing there. He didn't look sorry or ashamed. He was standing there just as if he'd done nothing.

"There you are. Prepare to die. You are a very bad man, whoever you are. You have ruined my family."

"Your family? I thought you didn't want them? I thought you didn't own them? You don't even know where they come from!"

"Don't you say that! You are saying that to hurt me!"

"Your family loves you very much, but you don't let them. Your wife could have left you a long time ago but she comes from a good and knowledgeable family. She tried to make you a better man but you wouldn't let her. You don't even know where the young ones you call 'things' come from. You put your penis, the thing between your legs, in her and you left part of yourself inside her. What you left are like little swimming fish. Those 'things' are from your body to hers, and they grow inside her, and then they come out already formed—a little one."

Qwunitun aimed his arrow at Xeel's and Xeel's said, "You can do that if you want, but the weapon will not harm me. You don't have to be angry at me and you don't have to worry about them now, my son. They are gone."

"How do you know that and why are you here?"

"I am here because your wife is always praying, calling for help for you and the children. But she never asks for help for herself. Her family prays for her also. They call me to watch out for her because they know I travel all over. With a blink of an eye, I appear wherever I am needed. That is why my name is Xeel's. Your family also asks for help. Right at this moment, her family is visiting your family."

"Why are they doing that?"

"Because they want to get to know your family better and both families are concerned about you and your own family."

"Now I am really mad. I will go and look for my family and beat them up and burn their feet because they deserve it."

"If you do that, you will never see them again. They will leave you and they will never return. But if you want them to come back, I will help you. I know deep down inside, you want them—but you want to own them. You cannot own anyone. You must allow them to be themselves. You want to be mean to them, but you must just love them."

Qwunitun had a sinking feeling in his stomach because he knew what Xeel's said was true. All of a sudden he realized he didn't want to live without his family.

"I am going to look for them because I want them. I want to be with them. I know that now. I hope they will forgive me. I am going to be a good father from now on. I know they are my children now. I never knew where the little ones came from before. I thank you; I thank you, Father, for opening my eyes and my heart. I know you did it in a way that would really open me up and make me realize how bad a father I have been and how bad a man I have been. I know I am qwuní, a thing that flies, but I also know I am a man."

Qwunitun was so excited now and he started to run around. He didn't go towards their little house because he knew they were no longer there. He knew they were going home to her village. But as he journeyed along the trails he couldn't find their scent; he knew their scent but he couldn't find it. He wondered if they were able to hide their scent, whether they were knowledgeable enough to do this. He always wondered about the eldest one. Maybe his son knew how to do this.

Qwunitun kept on looking and looking, going into the water, flying around, looking and looking. He felt very heavy. He knew that if he stayed on the ground, he would find them more easily. At night he stayed in the trees and during the day he stayed connected to the ground to see if the scent was there.

Early the next morning, he said to the trees, "You are helping them. You are looking after them and not me. Why?" He didn't receive an answer but this time he didn't get mad.

"Thank you for looking after them. They are very precious. I wouldn't want to live if I lost them, especially her." Qwunitun wasn't used to thinking this way and he thought, "Is that part of a prayer or am I really thinking this way?" The trees didn't answer him but they knew what he was thinking. Then he prayed to the water. He could see that the water was very clear, yet it seemed to stand up like sharp little heads coming up out of the water. "That is good, that is a good sign that they are helping me." He began to dance and sing "qwuní, qwuní, qwuní."

He knew where they were going now. He could smell them on the logs, hopping from log to log. It wasn't just her, it was all of them.

"Oh, my sons, I am so proud of you. You are taking care of your mother." The q̓ulé:q̓e' family started to fly around him, just about touching him, and he knew they were happy with him. Even though the q̓ulé:q̓e' were not speaking, they were guiding him, he knew that. "Yes, they are accepting me. They know how much I love my children and my wife."

Early the next morning, he could see them. The boys looked so big. They were running through the bush. They weren't flying because there was too much to pack. As he was coming over a hill, he became aware that he should have his scent go upwind, not downwind. At that very moment his eldest child dropped the pack he was carrying and took out his bow and arrow. Their mother was in the middle of her children as they surrounded her, protecting her. They had heard him from far away say that he was going to kill her and those ugly things she calls her children. That was the last they heard before they started their journey.

The eldest son said, "You will only be able to kill one of us, but not our mother. Before you load your arrow again we will kill you. Go away, we don't ever want to see you again. We don't want you to harm our mother and make her sad. We remember that you have always done this to her."

They were men now, they weren't children anymore; and this surprised Qwunitun. Some of them looked like her and some of them looked like him. What was the name of the big white one? He didn't even know their names! "I am not going to think about it, because it is terrible that I don't even know their names." When Qwunitun realized he was carrying his weapons, he dropped them quickly.

"I am not going to kill you. You are mine. You are a part of me. I can't say I own you because you own yourself. You can kill me now if you want to but I will always love you. Father Xeel's has taught me an important lesson. He taught me to open my mind and my heart and my very soul. I was selfish and angry and mean all my life but now I know a different way because our Father, the Creator, showed me that I was doing everything wrong. I have changed for you, for myself, for your precious mother. If it were not for her I would be dead, just bones and feathers on the beach. I don't know what love is but I know deep within me I want to hold you and help you, laugh with you and cry with you. Maybe that is what I didn't know before."

"That is what I've been wanting to hear for such a long time," Qu'le said. "Even in my deepest, worst moments I knew I couldn't leave you. You were like a little boy that I must look after and raise. But now I see you are different. My beloved children, this is your new father."

At that moment the youngest one looked up and said, "Mother, look way over there, coming from the point. There are people coming, singing and drumming." There were white ones, black ones, all colours. The white ones had black paint on and the black ones had white paint on so they all looked alike.

Qu'le said, "That is my family, the q̓ulé:q̓e̓. That is my mother and father, my grandmother and grandfather. And there is the qwuní father and mother, grandfather and grandmother—the whole family."

They all came closer, singing with their arms raised to the sky. Qu'le's family said, "We received your distress call and that is why we went to see Qwunitun's grandparents. We decided that we must all come to be with you. We have come to heal with you. We have not come to harm anyone. We have only come to help if we can. We are so happy to see that Qwunitun has grown up on his own."

The families hadn't been told about Qwunitun's change of heart but they just knew what was going on as they had received the message from the universe. The family said, "You were on your way to see us, you never lost the way. You never lost the way of communication. You learned to go up into the sky and see far away in your mind." They were hugging one another and dancing.

All of a sudden a great voice came. "I am so glad, my children, that you have found one another. I am so happy you are together." This is what Xeel's said to the families of qwuní and q̓ulé:q̓e'.

They all raised their arms and said, "Thank you, Father. Thank you for helping our children to heal and thank you for sending them home to us." The families were so happy to be together in one big family.

Qwunitun said, "We haven't got much but we have some dried meat and fish at our home. Our home is not big but we can make enough room for everyone. We haven't got too much to eat but we will stretch it. My beautiful wife can make beautiful food."

Xeel's, the Creator said to the group, "My son has a big deer just waiting for you. It is outside and his wife has already skinned it and it is ready to be cooked. The little pouches of 'anuw̓ can be shared with the cousins. Also there are baskets of dried berries."

The young women and young men offered to help prepare the food. The young people said, "You must sit and get to know one another again. We will do the cooking."

The families were all so happy, black ones and white ones, all chattering at the same time, showing one another how they could dance and sing. Some were singing "qaá, qaá, qaá" and others were singing "qwuní, qwuní, qwuní" and others were drumming on the skins and it all sounded so good. They were all there together and they were all so happy. A few of the younger ones had climbed on Xeel's shoulders, one of the smallest was sitting on top of Xeel's walking stick, and another was brushing his hair.

Qwunitun was one of the last to arrive at his home. A little one came close to him and held out his hand and Qwunitun took it. Qwunitun thought to himself, "This is the one that always had snot hanging from his nose but now he is grown. He is so clean, he smells good. I don't want to scare him, so I'll just hold his hand." They stood together holding hands while the others danced and sang. After a while Qwunitun said, "I want to know your name."

"My name is Qa' like the water. My mother says I am like the water."

"Please, my son, Qa', you'll have to tell me the names of the others."

"Mother's name is Qu'le but we call her Tl'useep because she likes flowers and puts them in her hair and it smells so good. She gathers plants when I am ill and she gives them to me and I feel better. The oldest one's name is Suṅtl?e'."

"Yes, I've heard you call him Suṅtl?e', the older one."

"The next one is called Pu'q'us, which means the white face. The little ones we call 'the two' are Pi'kwun and Sqe'eq." They kept on walking and talking and then they came close to the hut. Xeel's was there waiting.

"You have travelled quite a distance to be with your family and you have changed your ways to be with your family. You must love them very much."

"I grew up hating everyone, Father, but I would die for my wife and my children now."

"I can feel they love you very much as well. They have always wanted to be with you. They wanted you as their leader and you will be a good leader."

Qu'le had baskets of gifts to give away. She had enough to put on a big potlatch and she started to go around the house, giving away the gifts. She now felt great happiness. The sons also went around the house to distribute the gifts of necklaces and bows and arrows.

Qu'le saw that her youngest son was being helpful and making pi'kwun (barbeque sticks) from the ocean spray tree. This is the name she gave her son because he danced when she was making pi'kwun. She could see that food was being prepared for the families. The basket that holds water was filled with water and hot rocks to cook the food. The dried fish and even the dried clams were cooked in this water and this helped the juices to come out of the food.

One of the old grannies was walking around, coaching the children, telling the younger ones how to cook the food properly. There were dried berries and roots that were mashed up with a bit of water. They mashed the food for the old ones that had no teeth to chew with. They wove the fish onto sticks and cooked them.

While the families feasted, Qu'le still went around the house giving gifts, and she told everyone how they had worked to prepare these gifts. She had known a day would come when she would give them away.

Xeel's said, "I must leave you, my children. Someone is calling me."

The q̓ulé:q̓e' family said, "We must also leave now."

Qwunitun and his family thanked the Creator and everyone for coming to this day of celebration. As was the custom, the old ladies wrapped bits of food for the guests to take—dried clams, fish, meat, and berries. The family knew that Xeel's does not actually eat food, but he was given food to take as well. He likes to smell the food and savour the smell.

A young woman asked, "Is he alive?"

Qu'le put her wing up and said, "He can be anything. He is everywhere. Just think of him no matter where you are and his energy will be there to support you." They were whispering but Xeel's looked behind him because he could hear everything they were saying.

The q̓ulé:q̓e' family said, "We will leave some of the material goods we brought to help you build a bigger home."

One of the younger qwuní cousins also had a wife who was a q̓ulé:q̓e'. They were so happy together and they wanted to stay with Qwunitun and his family. The Elders said, "We want this family to stay with you. Their little ones will learn as yours have learned. Your little ones are knowledgeable and they have learned in a different way as they are away from all others. We will visit you and you in turn will visit us. The road is made now and it is made in happiness."

The family could see that Xeel's had disappeared. Also their families were leaving and they were singing "qwunií, qwunií, qwunií, qaá, qaá, qaá." They shared each other's songs now. The families were singing, dancing, drumming and hugging as they left Qwunitun and his family.

Hay ch q̓aʼ.

Speaking with Ellen about "The Marriage of the Seagull and the Crow"

THIS IS A story about learning to love and take responsibility, and also about the importance of teaching young children about compassion and the acceptance of others. The seagull son becomes angry and rebellious when his family arranges his marriage to a crow from a distant village. His family has never taught him to be a good husband or father, feeling there would be time for that once his wife arrived.

Unfortunately, by then it was too late. As a husband he is unfeeling and cruel to his wife and children. Xeel's, the Creator intervenes and helps the seagull to awaken his inner being and become more kind and loving. The turning point comes when the seagull finally realizes that he loves his family and wants to be with them. At the end of the story, the seagull husband is forced to look at himself and his actions when facing the fact that he may lose the family he has come to love. Up until this point, the seagull had thought only of himself and had been disconnected from himself, his family, and Xeel's.

At the beginning of the story, Grandfather Qwuní was contemplating the intermarriages that were taking place in his family. He knew that he didn't want this type of marriage for his grandson Qwunitun. It is the Creator's teaching that it is not right to marry someone closely related to you. Offspring from that marriage have the energies of both the father and the mother and these energies are too similar, which can bring about future problems for the children. Knowing this, the grandfather asked Xeel's, the Creator, for a sign as to what they should do. The grandfather knew that Xeel's was there to support him. All he had to do was pray and ask for help. Xeel's teaches that we are never alone; we do not have to decide everything by ourselves.

Grandfather Qwuní knew it was time to include his family and the village in his thoughts, so he began to plan his speech so his words would come out the right way. When Grandfather Qwuní spoke he always included his family and acknowledged their involvement. It was important to let his guests know that the loved ones around him were part of the proceedings and aware of the gathering's importance. He acknowledged the involvement of the community in his decision, saying he had asked Xeel's for a sign and received an answer: to not make the decision on his own.

The people from the village agreed it was important to have another family join theirs, and told Grandfather Qwuní they would support him in this decision. Today as well, we can see how important it is for family members and extended family to partic-ipate in major decisions; this is vital to the survival of a strong family.

Unfortunately, this was also a time of sad realiza-tion for Qwunitun's family. They realized that they hadn't taught their children about taking a mate, or about how to appreciate that person or treat the mate with respect. The family understood that this was extremely important, as the mate would be bringing the next generation into the family; however, they thought these lessons could wait until after the marriage. They didn't realize that by then it would be too late. Training about love, marriage, respect, sex, and birth should happen well before a mate is taken.

The lessons of life need to be discussed regularly before they will stick. It is the responsibility of the parents and extended family to teach these lessons. Children need to learn about communicating, appreciating, showing respect, accepting differences, caring for others, helping others, sharing, and being kind. The lessons can be reinforced when you move on to talk about love, finding a mate, commitment, sexuality, and birth. There is a limited amount of time to teach the young about mating, but huge problems can arise if you haven't talked about the differences between the female body and the male body, sexuality, and birth. Even though Qu'le was a different colour, she was still a young girl and she should have been treated the same as family. It should be taught before a new mate comes into a family that he or she should be accepted into the family and treated with respect. No matter what the circumstances, we must remember that this union will bring the next generation.

The qwuní family was now ready to travel to the village of the crow people. Qwunitun began to question many things. As they left their campsite in the morning, his family prayed to Xeel's that any leavings might be useful where they lay. This is an important teaching—to acknowledge your surroundings and to thank the area for letting you stay there. Then, as Qwunitun started to pray, he began to wonder why he was thanking that place for allowing them to stay there overnight, when he had been so angry and unhappy there. These prayers were confusing for Qwunitun because he recognized the proper way to do things, yet he wasn't fully trained. This could have become an opportunity for him to question himself, yet he allowed his anger to take over. It is easy to let our anger take over rather than look at ourselves and question ourselves. When we do this we remain stuck in the same place.

This could also have been a good opportunity for Qwunitun to talk to his Elders, but he felt that anything he said didn't matter anymore. The entire situation had been taken out of his hands. He was too angry to know what he was thinking. He had always been told what to do so he couldn't really think or decide for himself.

In today's world as well, this can be a problem. If children feel they do not have any control over themselves or their surroundings, they can become angry and rebellious. One solution is to simply discuss new situations with your children, give them the facts, and then give them some alternatives. It is important to show your support and love towards your children when they ask questions so they will feel comfortable questioning all kinds of situations. If they are always told what to do and how to do it they will have difficulty thinking and deciding for themselves. By offering children choices and alternatives, you can help them learn to make better decisions on their own, when they get older.

In the story, the seagull family arrived at the crow village and asked the crow Elders if they would give permission for the young woman named Qu'le to marry Qwunitun. Once the proposal was accepted, everything just seemed to happen. The grandfather arranged for Qwunitun to be brought to the platform. There was another seat there and Qwunitun realized it must be for his future wife. He wanted to be sick but he remembered the teaching: Remove yourself, you are not yourself.

Qwunitun knew how to remove himself mentally from a situation, and he had learned not to do things for himself and not to think for himself. Even when the family went hunting, he had been told what to do. Having a wife would be exactly the same. He would bring her home and have her there. He would not have anything to do with her or touch her. His cousins told him he would be touching her and sleeping with her, but he didn't know why he would be sleeping with someone he didn't like. Why would he want to be with anyone so ugly, so opposite from himself? Qwunitun was very angry with his Elders who had made all these plans.

This is a pitiful story but it makes you think. Does this happen in today's world? Perhaps a young woman gets pregnant and the young man doesn't love her. To him the relationship is just for sex. Once she is pregnant, he starts to think she is not like him but is the opposite of him, and he doesn't want to be with her. He becomes angry and rejects her. He might also think that he doesn't want to look after the baby when it is born. This happens today as it did in the past. This is why it is so important to teach our children at a young age.

Qwunitun felt powerless in the decision about his marriage. When they arrived back home, he began to pack because he had already decided he was going to leave. The grandfather knew there was something terribly wrong and he spoke to him about being a man now and having his own family. The grandfather knew that they had not talked to him about these things, so why did he think the situation would turn out differently, when his grandson had never been taught about mating? Qwunitun hadn't seen his parents have close contact and they never talked to him about intimacy and sex. He had only heard snide remarks from his cousins. He didn't even know if the red bottom of his new wife was for penetration or if there was another part for penetration. It looked to him like puckered red lips. From listening to his cousins, he wasn't sure if you kiss it or penetrate it. He really didn't know how to have sexual contact with a female. Was he afraid of having close contact, or of not knowing how to go about it? He knew that he got aroused but when he felt himself and looked at himself, he could only wonder where to put it. Wasn't it his parents' or grandparents' business to explain to him?

Qu'le tried to help Qwunitun by inviting him to be with her. She attempted to teach him and comfort him, but in the end all he could think about was himself. He thanked her for allowing him to comfort himself. Does this happen today, that young men and women are having sex just to comfort themselves, not thinking about the children who might be the consequence? Like Qwunitun, will they reject their children? Qwunitun felt that these "things," his children, were just something he must feed. He thought that Qu'le should go out and get her own food, as his own mother had done. He didn't think about where the food came from or who cooked for him.

There were so many things he didn't know, such as how to be kind to another human being. The teaching was just not there. He hadn't been taught how to be kind to someone different, especially someone of a different colour. When Qu'le brought home these "things," it just sickened him. It is important to remember that he didn't have any siblings. He was an only child and his mother was not able to have any more children. He was a spoiled brat who hadn't been taught how to look after himself, much less anyone else, or to respect women and other people who were different from him. He hadn't been taught how to look after others. He was only concerned about himself. If children aren't taught these basic lessons of Xeel's, the Creator, how will they know?

In today's world, single parents and divorce are commonplace. Sometimes in these situations the parents will be too tolerant and spoil the child, thinking that they do not want to add to his or her burden. Or they may be at work all day and feel they don't have time to teach their children. But children are like sponges. They have a desire to learn and understand. It takes only a few moments to talk to a child about caring for others and compassion in order for the child to understand. When you talk about caring and compassion another time, the teaching is reinforced. If you never talk to your children about such matters, how will they learn? We all will face a variety of situations in our lives and must have the necessary skills to deal with each new one. If we spoil children and protect them from the harshness of the world, we add to their burden in life. Children must be taught the necessary life skills in order to survive and thrive.

Qwunitun's oldest son was already starting to think about the differences in people. He could see the differences between himself and his siblings, and realized they were different colours and sizes because their father was so different from their mother. The mother Qu'le had been taught to respect and love others the way they were, and she knew it was important to love her children just as they were. Her own children had been trained to love and accept others no matter how they looked. This is how the teaching should be passed on, though in today's world it doesn't always happen this way. It seems we are not always taught to accept and appreciate others and their differences. By not teaching our children this lesson, we may actually be teaching them to shun people who are different.

We can see in the story that Qu'le's Elders were knowledgeable in every aspect of teaching, passing on the history, spiritual teachings, and culture of their ancestors. This made Qu'le a strong woman and ensured the survival of the next generation. Qwunitun, however, had a very different upbringing. His training had been started but it hadn't reached the same stage of development as Qu'le's. He did know about certain things but he was totally at a loss in other areas.

This was shown very clearly when Qwunitun not only was unhappy about having children, but also about having to feed them. He grumbled about his bad fortune when he encountered Xeel's at the cross-roads. Xeel's tried to talk to Qwunitun and help him but Qwunitun turned his back on Xeel's and walked away. Despite the fact that Qwunitun had been so rude, Xeel's helped him anyway and told him where to find the deer. The deer seemed to stand there offering itself to Qwunitun; it was easy to shoot it. Just after killing the deer, Qwunitun became arrogant, but then he remembered his teachings and became humble.

In the teachings, we are told to always be aware of the different events that happen to us. No matter how big or small an event, or where or when it takes place, you must be aware of how you feel. You must be able to recognize and name the feeling. When Qwunitun became arrogant after killing the deer, the Elders would have said, "Your arrogance is going to jump in front of you because you think you know it all and that there is nothing left to learn." If you don't learn the lesson when you come to the crossroad, you will have to face it again in the future. You will be running around in circles trying to learn it, but you will miss it because you didn't think it was important to pay attention to your surroundings. You have to go back to square one and work it out yourself. No one else can do it for you. If you see that you are always facing the same difficult situation in your life, there is a lesson to be learned. Remember to always pay attention to what happens around you; learn to recognize what it is, and to name it.

At times, Xeel's will try to make you see that you are not on the right path. You may know you are being helped, but you don't acknowledge where the help comes from. For example, imagine you have entered another space or dimension where Xeel's is helping you. Then suddenly you think, "I did that myself, look at how great I am." Then—zoom—you are outside the space. In the story, Qwunitun became arrogant for a moment, but then he became humble, acknowledging that he had been helped. So the teaching is to recognize that you are being helped, acknowledge it, and thank the Creator the moment you realize it.

Qwunitun was often angry with his family and kept calling them down and belittling them. He felt he was overworked and he no longer wanted to feed them. When he put the ʼanuẃ into small packages for his children, he was full of anger. When he threw them at his children, the packages were transformed into packages of rock. It was a harsh lesson but it had to be harsh to awaken Qwunitun's inner self. He had to be taught to think about the feelings of others, but he remained untouched by this incident, still cold-hearted and mean.

Then Xeel's transformed the deer into a stump in an attempt to awaken Qwunitun's inner self. Again, Qwunitun disregarded the message. He was still angry and said he would kill Xeel's. Misfortune had been brought to Qwunitun, but he didn't stop and look at the situation or question it. He became angry with everyone around him, including Xeel's.

Many of us have come to that same crossroads in our lives, when we realize that what we have in the physical world is not what it appears to be. We may hope that the objects we acquire will be a blessing and create peace and harmony, but so often they only bring negative emotions such as grief, anger, and rebelliousness. This is the time to stop and look at what is happening and pray to the Creator for change. In times of distress, the immediate reaction may be one of anger and rage. This prevents us from going within ourselves, looking at ourselves, and allowing ourselves to see what needs to be changed.

Instead of doing this, Qwunitun decided he was going to find Xeel's and kill him. When he came upon Xeel's again at the same crossroads, Qwunitun noticed that Xeel's did not look sorry or ashamed. Qwunitun continued to be self-centred and angry and had not learned anything at all. Xeel's had tried to help Qwunitun to change by awakening his inner self, but this hadn't worked, so he now began to teach Qwunitun more directly.

He taught Qwunitun where the children came from, and that these children were a part of his body as well as Qu'le's. He explained that when Qwunitun slept with Qu'le, he left a part of himself inside her. He told Qwunitun that because of his actions he could lose the family that he had never loved or cared for. Xeel's offered to help him if Qwunitun was willing to change, and if he really wanted them back. Xeel's knew that he must be very clear in this teaching so that Qwunitun would not move on to make another mistake.

"You want to own them," Xeel's said to Qwunitun, "but you cannot own anyone." He explained that Qwunitun had to allow his family to be themselves and to just love them for who they were. Qwunitun had been so caught up in his own world and how it revolved around him that he hadn't even thought that he could love his family, or considered that he might be able to change his ways. All of a sudden he had a sinking feeling in his stomach because he knew what Xeel's had said was true. He realized that he did not want to live without his family, and that he had to go out and look for them.

In our lives, in everything we do, there are crossroads we must face. There always seem to be four roads, four choices. Which one are we going to take? Does the lesson show us that there are always different roads we can take in any given situation? When deciding whether to take the light road, the dark road, the hot road, or the cold road, we must first be able to recognize the differences. And we must consider that we might be putting ourselves into jeopardy if we don't abide by the rules.

Qwunitun remembered to thank Xeel's for opening his eyes and heart, and making him see what a bad father he had been. He was so excited about finding his family that he immediately started to run around and get ready. He had never felt this way before—excited, happy, and eager. He knew his family had left him and that they were going home to Qu'le's family and village. As he journeyed along the trails he could not find his family's scent. All of a sudden Qwunitun realized that the trees were helping his family by hiding them. He had never known how very precious his family was, and now he didn't want to live without them. Qwunitun wasn't used to thinking this way, and he asked himself whether he was saying part of a prayer, or whether his thinking really had changed. Once he had chosen this new path, it seemed that the environment was there to support him. The trees and water had heard his prayers and they seemed to be helping him. Even members of the q̓ulé:q̓e' family, her family, started to fly around him to show they were accepting him because of his change of heart.

Qwunitun followed the scent of his family and finally he found them. His children were prepared to protect their mother with their own lives. Qwunitun then realized he was carrying weapons, so he dropped them quickly and asked them to accept that now he really loved them for themselves, and would love them always. He confessed that he had been selfish and angry all his life, but that Father Xeel's had taught him to open his mind and heart. He acknowledged that Qu'le was responsible for his still being alive, not just bones and feathers on the beach. Now he wanted nothing but to be with his family, hold them and help them, laugh and cry with them.

This was a time for rejoicing. Qu'le and the children had waited for this moment for a long time. Both the seagull and the crow families joined the festivities. There was drumming, singing, and sharing of food. Qwunitun offered what little food they had and invited everyone to join them at their small home. Once Qwunitun had awakened his inner self and accepted his wife and children with love, and accepted Xeel's with love as well, the packages of 'anuẃ and the deer were transformed back to their original state. Qwunitun was shocked to hear from Xeel's that this transformation had happened.

The Creator can teach in a harsh way, but then he brings forth a loving, kind end to the story. Qwunitun hadn't really understood about praying. He had believed that he was the masterful one, and to be a man he shouldn't ask for help in prayer. He didn't have any feelings at all, for anything. The lessons of Xeel's had to be harsh in order to get Qwunitun to understand. In today's world we, too, need to pay attention when these things happen. We must remember to pray for help, for others and for ourselves.

The story shows that the children were more advanced in their teachings than their own father. Qu'le had taken the time to train them to show respect for all living and non-living things in the world. She had trained her children very well. Qwunitun had taken no part in teaching his own children, and when the family was reunited, he even had to ask his sons' names, getting the smallest one to tell him the names of his brothers. In a sense, Qwunitun became like a child, learning from the little one. Instead of becoming the new father and feeling that he must teach them and that they must listen, he asked his children to teach him. He had opened the lines of communication and become humble.

At the end of the story when Xeel's and the relations had left, there was a time of happiness and celebration, and an end to the time of loneliness and sadness for Qwunitun and his family. Now one of Qwunitun's younger qwuní cousins also had a wife who was a q̓ulé:q̓e'. They were so happy together that they wanted to stay with Qwunitun and his family. This was the start of an extended family, and Qwunitun and his little family would not be alone anymore. Qwunitun had also opened the road to Qu'le's family, inviting them to visit again and promising that his family would go to visit in turn. When the relations were leaving they were singing, "qwunií, qwunií, qwunií, qaá, qaá, qaá." They shared each other's songs now. Everyone was singing, dancing, drumming, and hugging.

Now Qwunitun would never again feel alone as he had in the past. He had allowed the Creator to teach him and accepted the Creator's teachings. He found kindness and love for his family in his heart, and also for himself. He felt as though he belonged to his family and extended family.

He now believed in the Creator and knew he had the Creator to rely on if anything should happen to him again. He knew that Xeel's was there to help him and support him. All he had to do was pray and ask for help.

GRANDPA TOMMY SPEAKS

How do you know when your feet go into the water?
Do you know when you take them out of the water?
What is it telling you?
Are you going to wipe them?
Do you know how to wipe them?
How will it feel when you put them on Mother Earth?
Can you feel it when you put them on Mother Earth?
Is He telling you how to do it?
Look and you will see. Listen and you will hear.
Look and Listen and He will tell you.

Hul̓q̓umín̓um̓ Glossary

ʼanuẃ • fat around deer kidney; deer fat

aa siʼém̓ • my dear one

aa si:ʼém̓ • my dear people

ćeẃiʼ • old clam shells; china (dishes), clam or oyster shell

chuchíʼq̓un • mink

ʼe:yt • cod; lingcod

ʼey̓x̌alʼlh • baby crab or little crabs

eetsun aw ee • I am here

hay ch q̓aʼ • thank you

hewt • rat

k̓wal̓uxw • dog salmon

le:l̓wusl • seating place; also benches, or sleeping platforms

lelum̓ • house

men • father

nem?ts tse? aw? sou?q?thamu' • we are going to look for you

nikw or **nikwiye'** • aunt, uncle, parent's cousin; used when addressing the person

nucím • why

pi'kwun • barbecue sticks; the name of one of Qu'le and Qwunitun's sons

pu'q'us • the white face; the name of one of Qu'le and Qwunitun's sons

q̓ulé:q̓e' • crow

q̓ullhánumucun • killer whale

q̓uyémun • clamshells or seashells; any type of bivalve shells when piled up together

qa' • water

qa:nlhp • arbutus tree

qwuní • seagull

qwunus • grey whale

s'uye?q • descendants

Shuyulh • older brother, sister, cousin; also a name meaning "the older one"

si'ém • honoured person, respected one

si:'ém • honoured people, respected ones

silu • grandmother or grandfather; grandparent's sibling or cousin

situn • basket

siyéẏu • my dear friends

sk̓waẇus • water baskets

slheyk'um'ews • breath of the body

smuyuth • deer

spa:l̓ • raven

spoo • shit

sq̓umul̓ • paddle

sqe'eq • youngest boy; the name of one of Qu'le and Qwunitun's sons

stuywut • north wind

sun̓tl̓ʔe' • eldest brother, sister, cousin

tq̓as • rock cod

tatalhum • flea

thaaq • big heads

thul̓shutun • mat

thuqul̓shúnum̓ • rainbow

Tl'useep • a girl's name meaning yarrow (or a word meaning licorice fern)

tumulh • red ochre

tuṅcáluqw • west wind; lots of water

tuṅwuq̓w • east and south wind

tuqwtuqw • red snappers

'umut • to sit down, to get out of bed

x̌ew̓s • new; to make things new

x̌i' • to appear, to become visible; to appear suddenly before you

Xeel's (also spelled **X̌e:ỉs**) • The Creator; the Transformer; the Changer

xwt̓lup • the deep; deep place

yuthust • to tell him/her

MIX
Paper from
responsible sources
FSC® C100212
www.fsc.org

Printed in January 2019
by Gauvin Press,
Gatineau, Québec